Graded Aural Tests
For All Purposes

Graded Aural Tests
For All Purposes

With suggested methods of working

Annie O. Warburton

Longman

Longman Group Ltd
London

*Associated companies, branches and representatives
throughout the world*

© Longman Group Ltd 1971

First published 1971

ISBN 0 582 32585 4

Printed in Great Britain by
Lowe & Brydone (Printers) Ltd., London

Contents

Preface   *xi*

Section I   Pulse, Accent and Time
1   Recognition of pulse   *1*
  (a) Marking the pulse in some way while music containing nothing but pulse notes is played   *1*
  (b) Clapping the pulse while music is played which consists of pulse notes with a longer note at the end of each phrase   *2*
  (c) Clapping the pulse while music containing varied rhythmic patterns is played   *2*
2   Duple and triple time   *4*
3   Duple, triple and quadruple time   *6*
4   Simple and compound time   *8*
  (a) Stating whether the time is simple or compound: beats divided into into two or three equal parts only   *8*
  (b) As for (a) but the beats divide in other commonly-used ways   *9*
  (c) Stating whether the time is $\frac{2}{4}$, $\frac{3}{4}$, $\frac{4}{4}$ or $\frac{6}{8}$ *10*
  (d) Recognising $\frac{2}{4}$, $\frac{3}{4}$, $\frac{4}{4}$, $\frac{6}{8}$, $\frac{9}{8}$ and $\frac{12}{8}$ time   *11*
  (e) As for (d) but the passages include irregular divisions of the pulse   *12*

Section II   Rhythm Patterns
Reproduction; identification of note values; writing from dictation   14–19
1   Note values confined to ♩, ♪, ♩., ○ and ♫   *19*
  (a) Two bars of $\frac{2}{4}$ or $\frac{3}{4}$ time   *19*
  (b) Two bars of $\frac{3}{4}$ or $\frac{4}{4}$ time   *20*
  (c) Three bars of $\frac{2}{4}$, $\frac{3}{4}$ or $\frac{4}{4}$ time   *20*
  (d) Four bars of $\frac{2}{4}$, $\frac{3}{4}$ or $\frac{4}{4}$ time   *20*

2   The addition of ♩. ♪   *21*
  (a) Two bars of $\frac{2}{4}$, $\frac{3}{4}$ or $\frac{4}{4}$ time   *21*
  (b) Three bars of $\frac{2}{4}$, $\frac{3}{4}$ or $\frac{4}{4}$ time   *22*
  (c) Four bars of $\frac{2}{4}$, $\frac{3}{4}$ or $\frac{4}{4}$ time   *22*
3   $\frac{6}{8}$ time. No note shorter than a quaver   *23*
4   The addition of semiquavers in $\frac{2}{4}$, $\frac{3}{4}$ or $\frac{4}{4}$ time   *24*
  (a) Comparisons between ♩. ♪ and ♩.♪   *25*
  (b) The addition of ♫♫   *26*
  (c) Other patterns using semiquavers   *27*
5   $\frac{6}{8}$ time, using semiquavers   *28*
  (a) The addition of ♩.♫   *28*
  (b) Other patterns using semiquavers   *29*

6 The addition of syncopation and triplets in $\frac{2}{4}$, $\frac{3}{4}$ or $\frac{4}{4}$ time *30*

7 The addition of syncopation, duplets and quadruplets in $\frac{6}{8}$ time *32*

8 $\frac{9}{8}$ time *33*

Section III   Pitch Tests: One to Five Single Notes

Reproduction; identification of pitch; writing from dictation 34–37

1 Singing the tonic at the end of a phrase *37*

2 Any one of the first five notes of the major scale *37*

3 Any note of the tonic chord of a major key *38*

4 Any one note of the major scale *38*

5 Saying which is higher or lower of two, or highest or lowest of three *39*

6 Two to five notes of the major scale *39*
   (a) Notes of the tonic chord only *39*
   (b) Stepwise movement and leaps between notes of the tonic chord *40*
   (c) Any notes *41*

7 The minor scale *42*
   (a) Any one note *44*
   (b) Three to five notes *44*

Section IV   Melody

Reproduction; identification of pitch; writing from dictation 46–49

1 Two-, three- and four-bar melodies in easy major keys; $\frac{2}{4}$, $\frac{3}{4}$ or $\frac{4}{4}$ time; no note shorter than a crotchet *49*
   (a) Melody lying between doh and soh, and starting on doh; keys C, G and F major *49*
   (b) Pentatonic scale; keys C, G and F *51*
   (c) Complete major scale, but the only leaps are between notes of the tonic chord *52*
   (d) As for (c) but also including any leap of a third *54*

2 The introduction of quavers and easy leaps, in easy major keys *56*
   (a) Two- and three-bar phrases *56*
   (b) Four-bar phrases *58*

3 The introduction of dotted notes and more difficult leaps *60*

4 Easy four-bar melodies in $\frac{6}{8}$ time, easy major keys *60*

5 Easy four-bar melodies in easy minor keys *61*

6 More-difficult four-bar melodies in any major key *62*

7 More-difficult four-bar melodies in any minor key *63*

8 Five- to eight-bar diatonic melodies *64*

9 Five- to eight-bar melodies containing chromatic notes *65*

10 Eight-bar melodies containing modulations *67*

11 Nine-to twelve-bar melodies containing modulations *69*

Section V Intervals

1 Reproduction of upper and lower notes of an interval, played harmonically *71*
   (a) Consonant intervals only (third, fifth, sixth and octave) *71*
   (b) Consonant and dissonant intervals *72*
2 Recognition of the size of an interval (number only), heard melodically or harmonically *72*
   (a) Consonant intervals only (third, fifth, sixth and octave) *72*
   (b) Consonant and dissonant intervals, omitting the tritone *72*
   (c) Any diatonic interval from the tonic of a major key *74*
   (d) Any interval of a major key, given the tonic *74*
3 Recognition of the size of an interval (number and quality) heard melodically or harmonically, without relation to a key note *75*
   (a) Major and minor third *75*
   (b) Major and minor sixth *76*
   (c) Major and minor second *76*
   (d) Major and minor seventh *77*
   (e) Perfect fourth, perfect fifth and tritone *77*
   (f) Any interval within an octave *78*
4 Naming and writing down the notes of an interval, given the key *78*
   (a) Diatonic in a major key *78*
   (b) Diatonic in a minor key *79*
   (c) Intervals which are formed by chromatic notes in a major or minor key *79*

Section VI Two-Part Tests

Reproduction of either part; writing both parts from dictation; two parts in the treble, or one part in the treble and one in the bass *81–82*

1 A series of three to six intervals *82*
   (a) Major keys *82*
   (b) Minor keys *83*
2 A two- or three-bar phrase in two parts *84*
   (a) Major keys *84*
   (b) Minor keys *86*
3 A four-bar passage in two parts *87*
   (a) Two parts on the treble stave *88*
   (b) One part on the treble stave and the other on the bass *90*
4 A five- or six-bar passage in two parts *94*
   (a) Two parts on the treble stave *94*
   (b) One part on the treble stave and the other on the bass *96*

Section VII Single Chord Tests

Various examination requirements *100*

1 Singing top, middle or bottom notes of a three-note concord *101*

2   Singing top, middle or bottom notes of a three-note discord   *101*

3   Stating the number of notes in a chord or two, three or four notes   *102*

4   Recognition of isolated triads in close and open position; singing any note; identification of the top note   *102*

    (a) Major and minor triads, root position   *103*

    (b) Major and minor triads, root position and first inversion   *103*

    (c) Major and minor triads, root position and first and second inversion   *105*

    (d) Major, minor, diminished and augmented triads, root position   *106*

    (e) Major, minor and diminished triads in root position and their inversions, and the augmented triad in root position   *108*

5   Recognition of the dominant seventh and its inversions; singing any note; writing down the chord, given one note   *110*

6   Recognition of a single four-part common chord as being in root position, first inversion or second inversion   *111*

    (a) Major common chords   *111*

    (b) Minor common chords   *112*

7   Recognition of I, IV and V and their inversions, as single chords in four-part harmony, after the tonic chord has been played   *113*

    (a) Major keys   *114*

    (b) Minor keys   *115*

Section VIII   Chord Progressions

Various examination requirements   *117*

1   I, IV and V in root position   *118*

2   I, Ib, Ic, IV and V   *121*

3   Primary triads and their inversions   *124*

4   Progressions containing major and minor common chords and their inversions   *126*

5   Progressions containing any diatonic triads and their inversions   *129*

6   Progressions containing any diatonic triads and their inversions, and the root position of the dominant seventh   *131*

7   Progressions containing any diatonic triads and their inversions, and the dominant seventh and its inversions   *134*

8   Simple progressions including modulation to related keys   *136*

9   Progressions including any diatonic chords, including suspensions, and modulation   *140*

10 Progressions including chromatic harmony   *141*

Section IX   Cadences

Various examination requirements   *144*

1   Perfect and imperfect cadences in root position   *145*

    (a) Tonic chord followed by I V or V I   *146*

    (b) A single melodic phrase followed by I V or V I   *146*

    (c) A single harmonised phrase followed by an imperfect cadence (any chord before V) or a perfect cadence *147*

    (d) A continuous passage containing two, three or four perfect or imperfect cadences *148*

  2 Perfect and plagal cadences in root position *150*

    (a) Tonic chord followed by a perfect or plagal cadence *151*

    (b) A single melodic phrase followed by a perfect or plagal cadence *151*

    (c) A single harmonised phrase followed by a perfect or plagal cadence *152*

    (d) A continuous passage containing two, three or four perfect or plagal cadences *153*

  3 All four cadences in root position *154*

    (a) Tonic chord followed by a cadence *155*

    (b) A single melodic phrase ending with a harmonised cadence *156*

    (c) A single harmonised phrase ending with a cadence *157*

    (d) A continuous passage containing two, three or four cadences *159*

  4 All four cadences in more elaborate forms *163*

Section X Key and Modulation

Various examination requirements *175*

  1 Recognising whether a passage is in the major or the minor mode *175*

  2 Recognising single modulations from a major key to the dominant or subdominant major or the relative minor *177*

  3 Recognising single modulations from a minor key to the dominant or subdominant minor or the relative major *184*

  4 Recognising single modulations from a major key to the five most closely-related keys *189*

  5 Recognising single modulations from a minor key to the five most closely-related keys *195*

  6 Recognising two or three modulations to related keys in a continuous passage *201*

    (a) Three modulations to related keys without a return to the tonic key in the middle *201*

    (b) Two modulations to related keys plus a return to the tonic key in the middle *210*

    (c) Three modulations to related keys plus a return to the tonic key in the middle *213*

Section XI Tests of General Musical Experience

Various examination requirements *221*

  1 Questions on instruments and orchestration *222*

    (a) Individual instruments *222*

    (b) Groups of instruments, or the way they are used *224*

2 Recognition of type of voice or of particular singer   *227*
3 Recognition of type of vocal composition or a particular vocal work   *228*
4 Recognition of type of chamber group   *229*
5 Recognition of a large instrumental group, or section of it, or of a particular movement from it   *229*
6 Recognition of form, structure or modulation   *230*
7 Recognition of dance forms   *231*
8 Recognition of period   *231*
9 Answering a number of varied questions on a piece of music, after several hearings of it   *232*
   (a) Solo vocal works (Folk songs)   *232*
   (b) Solo vocal works (Art songs)   *232*
   (c) Opera   *234*
   (d) Cantata and oratorio   *235*
   (e) Chamber music   *236*
   (f) Concertos   *238*
   (g) Orchestral works, other than concertos   *239*
10 Recognition of a hidden melody   *242*
   (a) Recognition of a melody when it appears below other melodies or harmonies in a classical composition   *242*
   (b) Recognition of a well-known hidden melody in the bass   *246*
11 Recognition of themes from works which have been previously studied   *255*
   (a) Recognition of themes by ear alone   *255*
   (b) Recognition of themes which are given both aurally and visually   *255*
   (c) Recognition of themes by sight alone   *256*

Section XII   Tests of General Musical Literacy

Various examination requirements   *257*
1 Adding speed and expression marks to a melody   *258*
2 Showing the structure of a melody   *260*
3 Adding time signatures and bar lines to an unbarred melody   *263*
4 Completing a melody of which the pitch and bar lines are given   *265*
5 Completing a melody of which the rhythm is given   *267*
6 Completing a melody, part of which is given   *270*
7 Detecting discrepancies between a copy of a melody and its performance   *271*
8 Answering a number of varied questions on a melody which is played, part of which is given   *274*

Preface

The fundamental task of every teacher of music, whether he is teaching a child-beginner at the piano, an advanced violinist, a school class or a church choir, is to train his pupils' ears in musical discrimination, so that they can perform musically and listen appreciatively. Unfortunately, some teachers are so concerned with the technique of teaching the instrument or voice, and with establishing a repertoire, that they fail to realise how much better they would achieve their object if they devoted some time to training in aural discrimination. If they are preparing their pupils for an examination, they reluctantly give an occasional ear test, and do not realise that ear tests do not take the place of ear training.

The more musical and intelligently perceptive the teacher is, the more he is likely to realise the basic importance of ear training. But in some cases, he has had little training in teaching it; and in other cases he is handicapped by the lack of suitable material.

This book attempts to fulfil both these needs by providing a graded course of training which gives hints and advice at every stage, and which provides sufficient material to cover every possible requirement. The teacher can sometimes find themes from the classics to use as additional material. But they can rarely be as well-suited for training purposes, as it is extremely difficult to find examples which are exactly geared to the stage of the pupil's aural ability and knowledge. Graded exercises of the kind given here are therefore essential.

There are plenty of books of ear tests based on the practical examinations of the various Examining Boards, but they often give little or no advice about methods of working. There are a few books on ear training methods, but usually they do not give enough examples. Also their authors are thinking, perhaps, of the requirements of one particular examination or type of music student, and tend to neglect others; and, in this connection, parts of the Advanced Level requirements of some G.C.E. Examining Boards, such as longer melodies with modulation, are hardly catered for at all. And the requirements of the C.S.E. examination have received very little attention, so far.

It was tempting, when writing this book, to try to relate every test to a particular examination, but it would have been very unwise to do so. Examinations are constantly changing, and the book would have been out-of-date within a year or two.

But what I have done, most carefully, is to look at all the present requirements of every public examination, and to see that they are all covered in this book, with sufficient examples in every case.

This book, then, fulfils two main purposes. It is primarily a course in ear training, with plenty of exercises of every kind, from the simplest to the most advance. It can be used by the piano teacher who is not preparing for any examination but who wishes to train his pupil's ear, and similarly by the class teacher who is trying to give his classes an all-round musical training, without any particular examination in mind.

Its second purpose, however, is to provide material for the many public examinations that pupils may take. These can be divided into three main types:

(a) *Oral tests for practical examinations*, from grade I to diploma standard. There are very many different requirements, but all are covered in this book.

(b) *Written dictation tests for G.C.E. O Level and A Level examinations, class music diplomas, College of Education examinations and university degrees*. There is a carefully graded selection of tests for all these examinations. At last, the teacher should have sufficient material.

(c) *The C.S.E. examination*. There are many different Examining Boards, which are run by the teachers themselves. They vary enormously in their requirements, and they are likely to undergo continual changes. A few Boards give some very simple melody and rhythm dictation tests of the conventional type and these are covered in this book.

But two main kinds of tests are also being given on gramophone records or tapes. The first kind is that of general musical literacy. The pupil is either given a copy of a melody or given parts of its rhythm or pitch on lined music paper. He can be asked to add such things as expression marks, phrase marks, time signatures and bar lines, or more of the melody or rhythm; and to detect alterations of detail.

This kind of test, in which one piece of music serves as a test of the recognition of a number of different musical features, is considerably harder than a test which is specifically written for a particular purpose, containing perhaps very easy rhythm patterns or very easy melodic shapes. Eventually teachers will perhaps build up stocks of gramophone records or tapes containing tests set in previous years' examinations. But some tests of this type are given here.

The second kind of test is that of general musical experience. The pupil answers general questions on the type of music heard on a record or tape, on its themes and its general musical texture, and no music notation is involved. The resourceful teacher can apply these kinds of questions to many of the records his pupils hear. But he may be glad of advice as to how to go about it, and also of some examples that will save his time in devising his own. Again, however, a collection of previously set examination records or tapes will, in time, become the chief material used.

Section XII, Tests of General Musical Literacy should have logically come before Section XI, Tests of General Musical Experience, in this book. But they have been changed round, so that the section involving printing in two colours comes at the end, which is easier for production purposes. Section XII is intended for the teacher only. The pupil must be provided with that part of the score which is printed in black in the book, so that he can add the necessary marks to it.

There are two pieces of advice that should be given to all teachers who are preparing their pupils for public examinations. The first is that they should study carefully the *current* syllabus, to be sure there are no changes from the previous year, and that they are giving their pupils the right kinds of tests. A book which states that a certain test is for grade IV or O Level is dangerous, because it may not exactly fit the requirements, or the requirements may have been changed.

Secondly, they should obtain some of the tests previously set in the examination for which they are preparing their pupils and use these as models, rather than those in any text book—though a text book can provide much useful additional material, when once the standard requirements are related to it.

Finally, though this book will probably be mainly used by teachers, it can also be used with advantage by the pupils themselves. They will find the methods of working helpful; there are many suggestions for self-help; and pupils can quite often give tests to each other and thus save the teacher's time. There are enough examples in this book for the use of both teacher and pupils.

Section I
Pulse, Accent and Time

1 Recognition of Pulse

It should not be taken for granted that everyone can recognise or reproduce a steady pulse in music. Obviously the young child needs practice in this, but many an older person is not consciously aware of the regular pulse underlying varied musical rhythms; and some find difficulty in keeping a steady pulse in their own singing or playing.

Bodily rhythmic movement is the obvious method of training the young child. The older student can be asked to clap the pulse while music is played to him.

(a) Marking the pulse in some way while music containing nothing but pulse notes is played

The student may stop clapping the pulse when the long note occurs. This probably shows an instinctive sense of phrase, but he must be made to realise that the pulse continues throughout the long notes.

1 Allegro

2 Largo

3 Andante

Sonata Op. 14, No. 2 Beethoven

(c) Clapping the pulse while music containing varied rhythmic patterns is played

Some students may clap the rhythm instead of the pulse, and the distinction between the two must be pointed out.

In addition to the examples given on the next page, any other examples, given in this book or elsewhere, may now be used.

1 Vivace

2 Moderato

3 Vivace

4 Lento

con 8

2 Duple and Triple Time

The student should first mark the pulse. Then he should listen for the strong beats and say 'one' to himself each time **they occur**. He should then continue to count the pulses (1 2 or 1 2 3) until **he** hears the next strong beat. Some students find difficulty in recognising accent; others may count the number of notes heard, rather than the pulses.

Some examinations require the student to beat time as a proof of recognition. The movement should clearly show the exact moment of each beat but, at the same time, it should have a rhythmical swing and not be 'wooden'. The 'down' beat should be strong and definite.

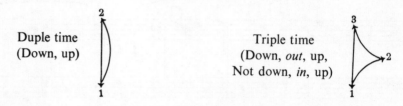

Duple time
(Down, up)

Triple time
(Down, *out*, up,
Not down, *in*, up)

Exercises in duple or triple time given in part 1 may be used again for this purpose, before going on to the following exercises. Exercises 9–12 are in compound time. Assuming that the student, at this stage, is unaware of the difference between simple and compound time, it is no more difficult to distinguish between duple and triple time, whether the beats are simple or compound. But these examples can be omitted at this stage if wished.

Most examinations give a melody for this purpose. But the teacher can harmonise the melodies given below, if wished.

5

6

7

8

9

10

11

12

3 Duple, Triple and Quadruple Time

Duple and quadruple time are very much alike. And many compositions, even by great composers, are written in duple time when they should be performed in quadruple time, and vice versa.

There *is* a difference, however, when the music is correctly performed. The pulses in duple time occur as strong, weak; whereas in quadruple time they occur as strong, weak, medium, weak. The latter, therefore, has relatively fewer strong accents and is less 'jerky'. But even if the teacher is meticulous in producing the right amount of accent, it requires keen listening for the pupil to hear the difference. This is why some relatively advanced examinations only give oral and written ear tests in duple and triple time. And it is no great crime to hear or write music in duple time when it is really in quadruple and vice versa.

The movements for beating quadruple time are down, in out, up:

Notice that, in triple and quadruple time, the movement leading to the strong beat moves away from the body. This can clearly be seen by a choir or an orchestra, and helps in the recognition of the strong beat and in the counting of silent bars. Even the second beat in duple time normally has an outward as well as an upward movement, so that the same preliminary movement leading to the strong beat is recognised.

Any of the exercises given previously can be used again, but some more are given here, a greater number being in quadruple than in duple or triple time. Also the later exercises are more rhythmically elaborate, as they would normally be given to more advanced students.

Examples of the three kinds of time should be played in random order. Those in compound time, 9–11, can be omitted, if wished.

4 Simple and Compound Time

(a) Stating whether the time is simple or compound: beats divided into two or three equal parts only

It is often not realised that the aural difference between simple and compound time is purely a question of what happens *inside* each beat. For this reason, the student is asked to state in the first stages, (a) and (b) here, simply whether the time is simple or compound. He can then devote his attention purely to this matter, without having to decide whether the time is duple, triple or quadruple.

At a later stage, when rhythmic patterns or melodies are written down, it is imperative to recognise at once whether the beat is simple or compound: it is much more important than recognising whether the time is duple, triple or quadruple. A wrong diagnosis will result in the rhythmic pattern being wrong throughout.

The student should first recognise the pulse, and then carefully listen to what happens inside each pulse. The easiest methods are to say 'one two' or 'one two three' inside each pulse, or to say *ta te* or *ta te ti*. Providing that the counting or rhythm names are said *evenly*, one will fit and the other will not.

(b) As for (a) but the beats divide in other commonly-used ways

A student often says [♩ ♪♪ ♩ ♪], and does not realise that, though he has heard two sounds within each beat, they were not of equal length.

The other common mistake is to hear [♩. ♪] as [♩ ♪]. But in these easy examples, given below, there will be other divisions of the beat that should leave the student in no doubt as to whether the beat is simple or compound.

(c) *Stating whether the time is* $\frac{2}{4}$, $\frac{3}{4}$, $\frac{4}{4}$ *or* $\frac{6}{8}$

$\frac{6}{8}$ time is much more common than any other kind of compound time; and some examinations require no knowledge of any other kind.

The student should first listen to the divisions inside each pulse and decide, as in stages (a) and (b), whether the beat is simple or compound. If it is compound, then, at this stage it will be $\frac{6}{8}$. If it is simple, then he must listen for the recurrence of the strong beats, as in parts 1÷3 of this section, and decide whether the time is duple, triple or quadruple.

A difficulty that may arise here is caused by the similarity between $\frac{3}{4}$ and $\frac{6}{8}$.

For example: $\frac{3}{4}$ ♩ ♩ ♩ | ♩ ♩ | ♩. ♪♩ | ♩. ‖

played quickly sounds very like $\frac{6}{8}$ ♩♩♩ ♩ ♪ | ♩. ♩♩ ♩. ‖

played slowly. But there *is* a difference—the former carries more strong accents than the latter. However, when it comes to writing down a rhythmic pattern, either of the above versions will usually be accepted, unless the beat has been given beforehand.

In order to make the difference between two bars of $\frac{3}{4}$ and one bar of $\frac{6}{8}$ quite clear the pulse should be given beforehand, or the $\frac{6}{8}$ version should be played so quickly that it cannot be mistaken for $\frac{3}{4}$.

Any of the exercises in $\frac{2}{4}$, $\frac{3}{4}$, $\frac{4}{4}$ or $\frac{6}{8}$ given earlier in this book, which contain divisions of the pulse, can now be used as tests. Exercises in part 4 (a) and (b) will be found easier for this purpose than the earlier ones.

In addition a few are given here which contrast $\frac{3}{4}$ and $\frac{6}{8}$.

(d) Recognising $\frac{2}{4}$, $\frac{3}{4}$, $\frac{4}{4}$, $\frac{6}{8}$, $\frac{9}{8}$ *and* $\frac{12}{8}$ *time*

The crotchet or dotted crotchet is the beat in all the exercises given in this section: there is no point in giving other notes as the beat since the student is not, at this stage, concerned with the notation of rhythmic patterns, but purely with the recognition of duple, triple or quadruple simple or compound time.

Exercises 1–6 are concerned with comparisons of simple and compound versions of the same kind of time.

Exercises 7–10 compare $\frac{6}{8}$ with $\frac{12}{8}$. $\frac{12}{8}$ time is not often used by composers and is rarely given in an ear test. It is very difficult to recognise the difference between two bars of $\frac{6}{8}$ and one bar of $\frac{12}{8}$. Only the most meticulous playing on the part of the teacher and the most keen listening on the part of the pupil will produce awareness of the difference; and most examiners would accept the one for the other. For this reason few examples of $\frac{12}{8}$ time are given anywhere in this book.

Any exercises in which division of the beat occurs may now be used as ear tests.

11

7

8

9

10

(e) As for (d) but the passages include irregular divisions of the pulse

Triplets occasionally occur in simple time and duplets and quadruplets in compound. But as most of the beats will be divided normally the prevailing rhythm should be clearly felt.

These tests should only be given to more advanced students.

1

2

3

4

5

6

Section II
Rhythm Patterns

Reproduction of a rhythm pattern can be by clapping, tapping, singing or whistling. Clapping is the least good of these methods, as it is clumsy, tends to be inexact (particularly where short notes are concerned), and cannot show that a sound is held on—for example, it cannot differentiate between ♩ and 𝅗𝅥 at the end of a phrase. Tapping is a little better, because it is easier to tap short notes rhythmically than it is to clap them. But singing is is the best method, because accents and exact note lengths, both long and short, can most easily be shown in this way. If the test is purely a rhythmic one, the rhythm can, of course, be sung on one note, even though it has been heard as a melody.

Many students, particularly boys and adolescents of both sexes, go through a phase when they are shy about singing alone. But they should be encouraged to do this from the earliest stages, and should be told that, for this purpose, quality of voice is not being judged at all. They will have to sing (or whistle) when being asked to reproduce a melody; and the sooner that singing is accepted, as being the natural method of reproduction for all ear tests, the better.

The student should, from the earliest stages, be able to distinguish the pulse from the rhythm pattern. Therefore, although this involves the physical difficulty of doing two things at once, he should mark the pulse, in some way, at the same time. If he sings the rhythm pattern, his hand is free to mark the pulse by tapping on any convenient surface. This is easier and less clumsy than using the foot. Beating time, while reproducing a rhythm, is more difficult physically; and the number of beats in the bar has to be recognised before it can be done. But it is valuable at later stages; and it is required in some examinations.

Successful reproduction of a series of musical sounds of any kind, whether of rhythm or pitch or both, depends upon the cultivation of *memory*.

A good memory is absolutely fundamental to the development of musicianship; and there are cases when what is thought to be a poor ear is primarily a poor memory. Sounds must be remembered before they can be analysed; and a piece of music makes no sense to a person who cannot recognise the recurrence of a tune. So the good teacher uses every method he can think of to develop his pupil's memory, whether by means of the usual kinds of aural tests or in the singing or instrumental lesson.

The pupil, also, can do much to help himself. He must cultivate the ability to 'think' sounds without reproducing them aloud. Then he can sing tunes to himself at any odd moment of the day, thus recreating his enjoyment of music he knows, as well as developing his memory. Or he can make up little original phrases and then 'think' them back to himself. When he becomes more proficient and has learnt to link up musical notation with its sound, he can look at a melody or short and easy instrumental piece and memorise it before he performs it. Performance from memory should always be encouraged; and the pupil should attempt to reproduce music, heard perhaps at a concert or on the radio, on his own instrument. Playing by ear, in this way, contrary to some old-fashioned ideas, does nothing but good.

Obviously the pupil must learn to memorise and reproduce a rhythm before he goes on to the later stages of identifying its note values, or writing it from dictation. So practice in this must precede these later stages, whether it is actually required for an examination or not.

IDENTIFICATION
OF NOTE
VALUES
Some method of associating the sound of a rhythm pattern with a mnemonic is invaluable. Counting is not helpful with notes shorter than a beat; such methods as 'one-and-a' are inexact; and inventing one's own doggerel is unnecessary when the admirable system of French rhythm names is already available.

Most class teachers of young children use these freely; those with older children sometimes find their pupils think them babyish, particularly if they have not grown up with them; and some instrumental teachers have not discovered their value.

But a good teacher, presenting them sensibly, can soon convince pupils at any age and stage of their usefulness. They must always be sung rhythmically, and the sound must be associated with the sign. There is no need ever to *write* rhythm names: ♩ ♫ ♬♩ should sound like *taa tate tafatefe taa* to the pupil, but he writes the note values, not the rhythm names.

A table of the most common and useful rhythm names is given on the next page for reference purposes. But, of course, they are not meant to be learnt all at the same time. They should be introduced as each new rhythm pattern is learnt.

The tables assume that the crotchet or the dotted crotchet is the beat. This is always the case in simple oral tests; and dictation tests can always be written down in this way.

Should some other note be required as the beat, or should a student play or sing music with another note as the beat, he should still call the beat *taa*, and adjust the other names accordingly. For example, in $\frac{2}{2}$ time ♩ =*taa*; in $\frac{4}{8}$ time ♪ =*taa*; in $\frac{9}{16}$ time ♪. =*taa*.

If the student can say the pattern to rhythm names he can say ♩ ♫ ♬♩ consists of 'crotchet, two quavers, four semiquavers, crotchet', if required to do so, though some examiners will accept *taa tate tafatefe taa*. The latter can be said rhythmically, while the former can not.

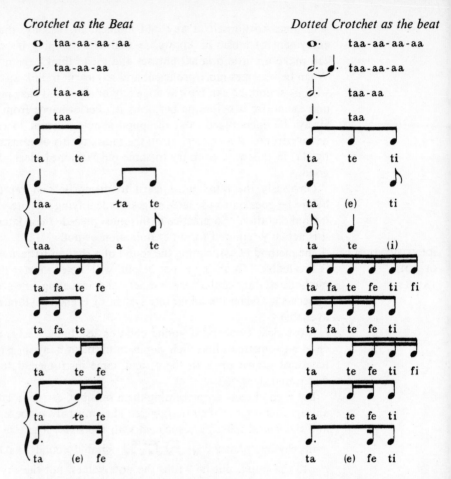

Crotchet as the Beat	Dotted Crotchet as the beat
taa-aa-aa-aa	taa-aa-aa-aa
taa-aa-aa	taa-aa-aa
taa-aa	taa-aa
taa	taa
ta te	ta te ti
taa ta te	ta (e) ti
taa a te	ta te (i)
ta fa te fe	ta fa te fe ti fi
ta fa te	ta fa te fe ti
ta te fe	ta te fe ti fi
ta te fe	ta te fe ti
ta (e) fe	ta (e) fe ti

WRITING FROM DICTATION

When writing from dictation the rhythm must be reproduced (i.e. memorised) and the notes must be identified (i.e. sung to rhythm names). But, in addition, the student must have a clear idea of the visual picture which the pattern makes. To help in this latter, and also to aid the memory, musical shorthand can be introduced. It brings in the muscular memory as an additional helpful factor, the hand moving the pencil in a kind of a dance, in time with the rhythmic pattern. Anyone who has experimented with the Somervell shorthand realises its value. One cannot write ♩ ♫ ♬♩ at the speed it is played, but one can do this with | ⅴ ⱳ |.

Here is a table showing the patterns for which shorthand is helpful, in simple and compound time. Somervell suggested treating $\frac{6}{8}$ time as six quaver beats, ♪♪♩. being written as | | | ⱨ. But, as $\frac{6}{8}$ time really sounds like two beats in a bar, and not six, the author has substituted a different shorthand on the next page.

16

When the student has progressed to more complicated rhythm patterns he will have outgrown the usefulness of shorthand; and it is even possible that he will not need it for compound time at all. But in the earlier stages of simple time it is invaluable.

Crotchet as beat

Dotted crotchet as beat

Let us suppose that the pupil has to write down the following:

It is helpful, in the earliest stages, to work in this way:

(i) *Listening*. Listen while the rhythm pattern is played (twice, if necessary) trying to say the rhythm names, mentally, to it.

(ii) *Reproducing*. Sing, clap or tap it, twice if necessary; and, in the first attempts, the rhythm names may be said aloud, if wished. (These performances must be continuous.)

(iii) *Getting ready to write*. The teacher quickly says 'Pencils ready', in such a way that the performances are not interrupted.

(iv) *Writing shorthand*. Pupils write down the shorthand. This *must* be in time with the performance. If they are late with the first note, they cannot catch up. They should write, while the teacher plays:

It is recommended that it should be written on a music stave, between the second and fourth lines, so that the sign for *taa*, | , cannot be confused with a bar line; and it is important that it is well-spaced-out, with room left at the beginning for the later addition of the time signature.

B

(v) *Checking*. The teacher now plays the rhythm again, while the pupil traces over what he has written, or has a second chance to correct or add to it, if necessary.

(vi) *Adding bar lines*. The teacher plays it again while the pupils trace over what they have written, adding the bar lines as they hear the accents ('A bar line is a thing you *hear*'). Then they add the time signature. The rhythm now looks like this:

(vii) *Translating into notes*. The pupil then translates the shorthand into musical notes, at a leisurely rate and in his best handwriting, writing each note *exactly* under its shorthand sign. The advantage of even spacing, rather than cramped writing, in the shorthand, will now be seen.

The final result will look like this:

As the pupil progresses some of these repetitions can be left out. And, when an examination is approaching, the teacher is advised to dictate the tests the number of times the particular examination requires, following also any given directions as to method. But shorthand is a help up to quite advanced stages, and certainly up to G.C.E. O Level.

Singing rhythms at sight is an essential part of training the link between the ear and the eye. This should be pursued at the same time as the ear tests, suitable material being found in class music books, or in music written for the particular instrument the pupil is studying.

The examples which follow are carefully graded into stages, and can be used for all three purposes mentioned above: reproduction, identification of note values, and writing from dictation. The teacher must decide how many are needed for each pupil or class, according to their ability or their examination requirements.

Some examinations start all their tests on the first beat of the bar. But anacrusic rhythm is more common and is just as easy, if pupils understand the principle of phrase lengths, the functions of the bar line, and realise that 'a bar line is a thing you hear'. The tests are freely mixed below: the teacher must choose what he requires. If desired, anacrusic tests can be played without the anacrusis, but the last note must be correspondingly longer.

Many elementary examinations, such as the C.S.E., confine dictation tests to rhythms wth no notes shorter than a quaver. For such examinations parts 1–3 of this Section are all that will be required.

At certain stages the teacher may find additional material from the tests given in Section I.

The examples are all given on a melody, as this is more musical than on one note, and most examinations now require it. But the teacher can, of course, play any of the examples on one note if he wishes, or an examination requires it.

In oral tests it is not customary for the beat to be indicated before the test is heard. But in written dictation tests the beat is indicated in most examinations. Teachers should read the syllabus to find the exact requirements, and study previously-set papers to discover the kind and the difficulty of the test required.

1 Note values confined to ♩, ♩, ♩., 𝅝 **and** ♫

(a) *Two bars of* ²⁄₄ *or* ³⁄₄ *time*

(b) *Two bars of* ³⁄₄ *or* ⁴⁄₄ *time*

Some examinations give tests in ²⁄₄ and not ⁴⁄₄ time or vice versa, because of the difficulty of distinguishing between ²⁄₄ and ⁴⁄₄ time (see Section I, part 3). The following tests assume that ²⁄₄ will not be given. But they can be interspersed with the previous set, if desired. And in later sets of tests the teacher can choose what is necessary.

(c) Three bars of $\frac{2}{4}$, $\frac{3}{4}$ *or* $\frac{4}{4}$ *time*

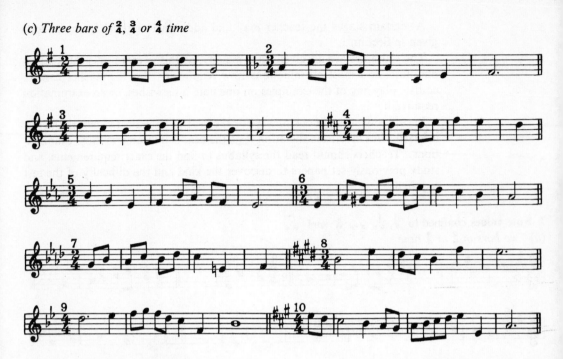

(d) Four bars of $\frac{2}{4}$, $\frac{3}{4}$ *or* $\frac{4}{4}$ *time*

Two bars are hardly long enough to establish a rhythmic shape, and are only of value in the earliest stages. Three-bar tests are often given for oral recognition because they are as long as the elementary pupil can remember and reproduce in one piece. But three-bar phrases are rather unusual and, in general, four-bar tests are more satisfactory. This is the usual length for elementary dictation tests. Four-bar phrases can be split into two sections, if necessary, both for oral reproduction and written dictation. A four-bar dictation test, dictated in two sections, may be easier to apprehend musically than a short two-bar test. And some teachers may prefer to start with these, rather than with two-bar and three-bar tests.

2 The addition of 𝅗𝅥. ♪

This rhythmic pattern often causes difficulty. It should first be shown as

𝅘𝅥 𝅘𝅥𝅮𝅘𝅥𝅮 = 𝅗𝅥. ♪   and the pupil should be made aware of the beat where
taa-*tate*   taa-ate

the dot occurs. When performing the rhythm he should be told to 'pull through the dot', giving a slight accent where the dot occurs. Rhythm names are a help in recognising the note values; the pupil says *taa-aa*, as he hears a sound lasting on to the second beat; then, just at the end of the beat he hears *te*, so the resulting rhythm name is *taa-ate*. The first sound is two beats *minus* a quaver, resulting in 𝅗𝅥. ♪ .

The shorthand is even more of a help when it comes to dictation. The pupil again says *taa-aa* while he writes ʰ . Then, just at the end of the second beat, as he is about to lift his pencil, he hears *te*, and adds to the sign ⁄ , thus producing ʰⱴ. He will then realise that he translates the shorthand into 𝅗𝅥. ♪ not 𝅗𝅥. 𝅘𝅥𝅮 .

(a) Two bars of $\frac{2}{4}$, $\frac{3}{4}$ *or* $\frac{4}{4}$ *time*

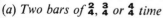

(b) Three bars of $\frac{2}{4}$, $\frac{3}{4}$ or $\frac{4}{4}$ time

(c) Four bars of $\frac{2}{4}$, $\frac{3}{4}$ or $\frac{4}{4}$ time

3 $\frac{6}{8}$ Time. No note shorter than a quaver

There are two principles that the teacher must explain to the pupil, and get him to learn. The first is concerned with sound: in simple time the beats divide into two; in compound time they divide into three. The second is concerned with notation: in simple time the beats are written as ordinary notes; in compound time they are written as dotted notes.

As $\frac{6}{8}$ is much more frequently met with than any other kind of compound time the first tests are confined to $\frac{6}{8}$, and the pupil can be told that this is the case.

The next stage is to mix $\frac{6}{8}$ tests with tests in $\frac{2}{4}$, $\frac{3}{4}$ and $\frac{4}{4}$. Any of the tests previously given in this Section can be used for this purpose. Unless the pupil is told the time signature (as happens in some examinations) he must first decide whether the beat is simple or compound. Otherwise the whole pattern will be wrong. From now onwards this is always the first question he must ask himself, when dealing with a rhythm (see part 4 (a), (b) and (c) of Section I).

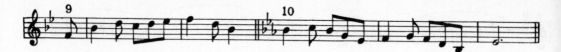

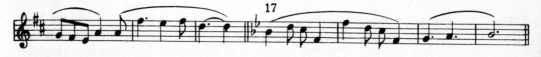

4 The addition of semiquavers in $\frac{2}{4}$, $\frac{3}{4}$ or $\frac{4}{4}$ time

When teaching a class it is helpful to write a table such as the following on the blackboard, and to point from one line to another at random, the class singing the rhythm names, until they become easy.

(a) Comparisons between ♩. ♪ *and* ♩♪

The most frequently-used rhythm pattern containing semiquavers is ♩♪.
It is much more common than ♫♫ , which is a rather quick pattern to
be used in a simple melody. But ♩♪ is often mistaken for ♩. ♪ . It should
be realised that the former occurs inside one beat while the latter is spread
over two beats. The exercises below are designed to give plenty of practice
in differentiating between the two.

In many simple rhythm tests ♩♪ is the only pattern using semiquavers;
and this is the standard of many G.C.E. O Level dictation tests.

(b) The addition of ♪♫♫

This pattern is easily recognised. Exercises 1–14 which follow use it as the only pattern requiring semiquavers, so they can be given before the (*a*) group above, if wished. Exercises 15–20 include both patterns.

(c) Other patterns using semiquavers

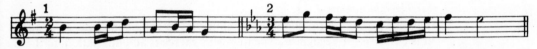

5 $\frac{6}{8}$ Time using semiquavers

(a) *The addition of*

The most common rhythm using semiquavers in compound time is . It is quite easy to recognise. The following exercises add this pattern to those already known.

The two- and three-bar tests are the kind that might be required for oral reproduction in a practical examination; while the four-bar tests might be given as dictation for G.C.E. O Level.

(b) Other patterns using semiquavers

  The two- and three-bar tests might be given for oral reproduction in the higher grades of practical examinations, while the four-bar tests might occur as dictation tests for G.C.E. A Level.

6 The addition of syncopation and triplets in $\frac{2}{4}$, $\frac{3}{4}$ or $\frac{4}{4}$ time

The tests that follow gradually become longer and more difficult until they are as difficult as any that are likely to be set in simple time in any kind of examination.

The two- and three-bar tests might be given for oral reproduction in the higher grades of practical examinations; the four-bar tests are similar to those given in some of the G.C.E. A Level written dictation tests; while the longer ones might be given as dictation tests for a class music diploma.

As before, rhythm names are a help, e.g.: ; and , with the names borrowed from compound time.

Rests are occasionally given in these tests. But many examinations do not set them. The performances of

and

are almost identical, because the last note at the end of the phrase is naturally shortened. But an answer giving either version should be equally acceptable.

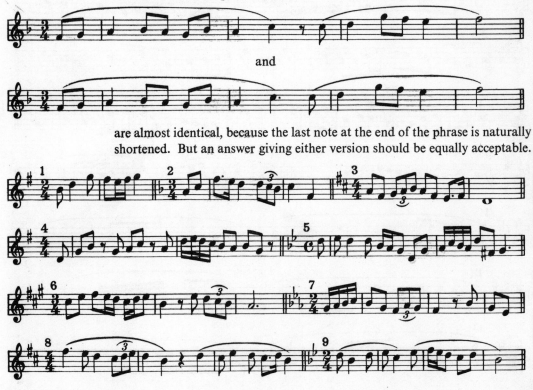

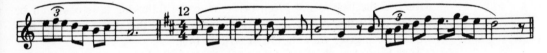

7 The addition of syncopation, duplets and quadruplets in ⁶/₈ time

Like the tests in part 6, these tests are as difficult as any are likely to be found. They should be mixed with the part 6 tests, so that the student has to decide whether the test is in simple or compound time before starting to write. If the beat is not given beforehand the following tests could all be written in ³/₄ time, producing twice as many bars. But if the beat has previously been given they should be written in ⁶/₈.

It is helpful to think of duplets as *ta te*, and quadruplets as *ta fa te fe*, whether the time is simple or compound. Rhythm names similarly help with syncopation, the 'a' vowel being said at the beginning of the beat, whether there is a new sound there or not.

8 $\frac{9}{8}$ Time

A few $\frac{9}{8}$ tests are given here for those who require them. No $\frac{12}{8}$ tests are given for dictation, because one bar of $\frac{12}{8}$ is indistinguishable from two bars of $\frac{6}{8}$, and it is unrealistic to expect students to hear the difference.

Section III
Pitch Tests: One to Five
Single Notes

REPRODUCTION

The reproduction of pitch tests varies from singing a single note in the most elementary examinations to memorising quite long melodies in senior examinations.

The comments about the use of the voice and the cultivation of memory, given in Section II, apply also to this section.

The pupil may be asked to reproduce a note or notes heard on the piano. The teacher can easily make up tests of this kind, but the order of difficulty given below is a useful guide.

If the pupil is asked to reproduce a series of six or more notes this is, in effect, asking him to memorise a melody; and the graded tests given in Section IV should be used.

In some examinations the pupil is given the tonic and asked to *sing* a certain note, perhaps of the tonic chord or of the major scale. As the pupil has to hear this note before he can sing it this more properly comes under the next heading of identification of pitch.

**IDENTIFICATION
OF PITCH**

Every teacher must be clear in his own mind that there are two quite distinct aspects of pitch in music.

The first is the actual pitch (or *absolute pitch*) of a sound, indicated by letters, plus sharps and flats: A, B♭, D♯, etc.

The absolute pitch of a sound depends upon scientific data. For example, vibrations moving at 440 cycles per second produce the note A, anywhere, on any instrument or voice.

Everyone who plays an instrument must, sooner or later, learn how to produce particular absolute pitch notes on his instrument, and to associate them with their names and their notation on the staff.

So it is natural that all instrumental teachers teach their pupils these facts as soon as possible.

But the second aspect of pitch is much more important in the development of musicianship. It is concerned with pitch *relationships*. Nearly all music that the pupil hears is in a major or a minor key; and the relationship of the notes in a key to the tonic and to each other (*tonality*), together with rhythmic relationships, are the fundamental bases of all tonal music. Our pupils are musical in so far as they are aware of these rhythmic and pitch relationships, and their ears must be trained to appreciate them, before they can fully enjoy music, or play with true musical perception.

Letter names are used for absolute pitch. But another set of names is required to express relationships, because it is something quite different.

Three ways are commonly used:

(a) numbers in relation to the tonic, 1, 2, 3, etc

(b) Technical names, tonic, dominant etc

(c) Sol-fa names.

The last method is more singable than the first two, and can be modified to express sharper and flatter notes. For example, it is much easier to sing, and therefore to think, doh soh fe soh than 1 5 4 sharpened 5, or tonic dominant sharpened subdominant dominant.

A small minority of people possess the gift of absolute pitch; and it is undoubtedly a useful asset, as they can recognise the pitch of any sound immediately and, provided they have had a training in rudiments, they can hear what musical notation sounds like.

But they do not necessarily have a good sense of relative pitch; and without this their performances will be insensitive and their appreciative understanding of music very limited.

So the good teacher sets out to develop a feeling for tonality in his pupils, whether he is teaching them singing, or how to play, or how to listen with appreciative understanding. And the earlier the teacher starts this training the better.

But no sensible teacher tries to teach anything without the use of names for his subject matter.

Quite a number of instrumental teachers, however, try to manage with the one set of names, the letter names, not realising that they cannot express relationships, and that relationships must be taught. The growing amount of instrumental teaching in junior classes—recorders, tuned percussion instruments etc.—is tending to encourage this, as the letter names have to be taught so early.

However, there really is no way out; there *are* two aspects of pitch; and two sets of names *must* be taught.

Ideally, relative pitch should be taught before absolute pitch, and before anyone learns to play an instrument. But the teacher who is anxious to get his pupils started on playing an instrument may begin with the absolute pitch names: it is inadvisable to teach both at the same time, as confusion may result.

But, whichever is taught first, the moment will come when the pupil should realise the need for the other set of names; and the two sets should then proceed side by side.

Sometimes the teacher has a resistance to sol-fa names, either because he managed without them in his youth or because he was taught them badly. Sometimes a pupil or a class has a resistance also, not realising the need for a second set of names. The good teacher must first overcome his his own resistance, if it exists, by doing some clear thinking on his own;

then he must overcome it in his pupils, if it exists, by convincing them of the need for two lots of names.

So it is recommended in this book that sol-fa names are used for melodic relationships in all pitch tests. They are always acceptable to examiners, though numbers are usually allowed as an alternative. The examiner may sometimes require them to be translated into their absolute pitch names in a certain key—often C, G and F in the earliest stages.

But sol-fa names, to be any use, must be very thoroughly associated with effects, so that the use of them becomes instinctive. In other words, constant practice is needed. This is training, rather than mere testing. Sightsinging practice and singing tunes to sol-fa names are invaluable. The pupil should eventually be able to sing notes, mentally, to sol-fa, singing silently from one note to another and analysing at the same time. (The teacher who needs further help in this matter may consult the author's *Graded Music Course*, books I-III.)

Here are the sol-fa names applied to C major and to the chromatic scale of C:

WRITING FROM DICTATION

In any pitch dictation test the most important thing is to *start* on the right note. The pupil should mentally sing doh (which he will have previously been given) while the test is played, and then sing from doh to the first note and write down its name in sol-fa. He should then mentally sing from there to the next note, and so on. He should write all the names of the notes in sol-fa over the staff before applying them to the particular key, checking that they really do sound like the name he has written, te sounding like te, doh sounding like doh, and so on.

If, for example, he hears: he writes

and then puts the notes on the staff afterwards.

36

Some examinations start every test on doh. The tests of two or more notes given in this section all start on doh, me or soh. If the teacher wishes he can add doh at the beginning to those that start on me or soh.

All the exercises given in this Section, except those given in parts 1 and 5, can be used for reproduction, identification or writing from dictation. A few tests contain an odd note which is too high for the average pupil to sing easily, and these should be omitted, played an octave lower or transposed, when reproduction is required. They are included because pupils should be able to identify these notes, or write them from dictation.

1 Singing the tonic at the end of a phrase

This is a useful preliminary in the development of a sense of tonality, and it is required in some elementary examinations.

A few graded examples are given here. If more are needed, many exercises in other parts of the book can be used, the teacher omitting the last note, and the pupil supplying it.

2 Any one of the first five notes of the major scale

Some teachers and some examinations start with stepwise movement, doh ray me fah soh, while others start with the tonic chord, doh me soh doh¹. Each method has much to commend it; and examples of both methods are given here.

In the following tests the pupil should sing, mentally, by step from doh up to the note which is given. These tests are so simple that the teacher can easily make up as many more as he requires. Some examinations confine these tests to the keys of C, G and F.

The tonic should be played before each note.

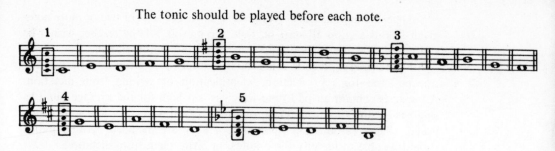

3 Any note of the tonic chord of a major key

The teacher who starts with doh me soh doh' may find that his pupils think of doh me soh doh' as upward *steps*, and at a later stage confuse doh me soh with doh ray me. Whichever is taught first a moment must come when the two effects doh me soh and doh ray me are compared; and one should frequently be given after the other, as in part 6 (*b*), until the pupil is sure of the difference. Practice in singing the major scale followed by the tonic chord will help.

The following are the kind of tests the teacher can make up for himself. Some examinations confine this test to the keys of C, G and F.

The tonic should be played before each note.

4 Any one note of the major scale

If the pupil has previously had practice on doh to soh, or doh me soh doh', he should now concentrate on the sounds he has not yet learnt. The tonic should be played before each note, and the pupil should learn to sing mentally up (or down) from doh to the given note.

Again, the teacher can easily make up these tests for himself; but a few are given here. Tests in dealing with notes outside the octave doh to doh', as at 5–7 below, should be given at a later stage.

5 Saying which is higher or lower of two, or highest or lowest of three

This test is sometimes required in elementary examinations. The notes concerned should, at first, be far apart, and then gradually become closer together. The following are graded examples of the kind which might usefully be given, and the teacher can easily make up more.

6 Two to five notes of the major scale

(a) *Notes of the tonic chord only*

The first tests should consist of doh me soh doh'. Of these, doh' me is the most difficult to recognise and sing. Later, notes outside the range of this octave may be added.

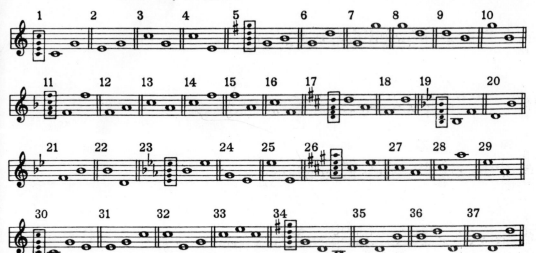

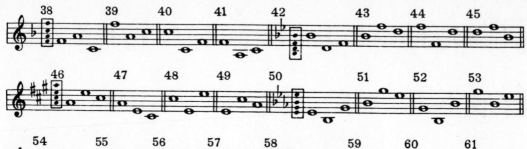

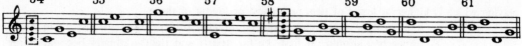

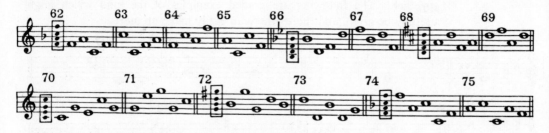

(b) Stepwise movement and leaps between notes of the tonic chord

Some examinations, such as those of some C.S.E. Boards, confine their pitch tests to this requirement.

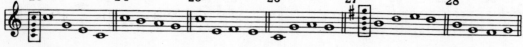

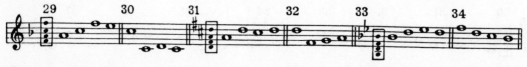

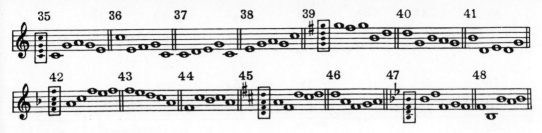

(c) Any notes of the major scale

These, like other tests, should be carefully graded. An interval with a leap containing lah seems to be the most difficult to recognise. The size of the interval has very little to do with it. For example, doh soh is one of the easiest intervals to recognise, while ray lah is one of the most difficult; yet both are perfect fifths. Ray lah, me lah and lay ray' usually cause trouble.

The key that is used makes no difference to the difficulty of the test—assuming that the key is known. Exercises 1–42 below are in the keys of C, G and F, because some examinations confine their tests to these keys. Exercises 43–56 are in keys with two sharps or flats, while exercises 50–70 have three sharps or flats.

If the pupil is asked to give the letter names, or to write the test down on the staff, he should think the sounds in sol-fa and then translate them into the particular key.

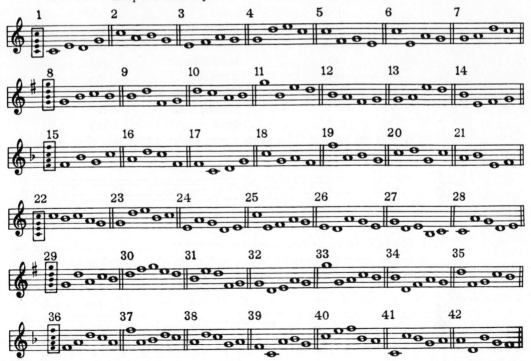

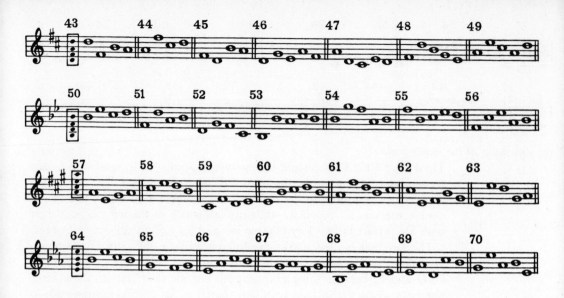

7 The Minor scale

There are two methods of using sol-fa names for the minor scale, the doh minor and the lah minor. Both are shown below, for the harmonic minor.

	DOH MINOR	TECHNICAL NAMES	LAH MINOR
1	doh	tonic	lah'
2	ray	supertonic	te'
3	maw	mediant	doh
4	fah	subdominant	ray
5	soh	dominant	me
6	law	submediant	fah
7	te	leading note	se
8	doh'	tonic	lah

Here is the scale of C *harmonic* minor, showing both sets of sol-fa names:

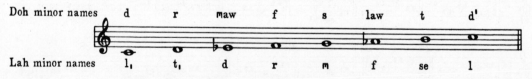

The *melodic* minor scale smooths out the augmented second between the sixth and seventh degrees by raising both notes when ascending and lowering both notes when descending, thus:

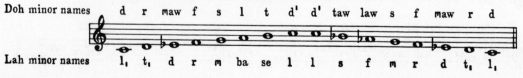

42

The lah minor method considers the minor scale as a subsidiary of its relative major, rather than as a scale in its own right, and therefore approximates more closely to written notation, in which C minor borrows the signature of E♭ major. In other words, it is thought of *visually*.

The doh minor corresponds to the numbers and the technical names, the first note of the scale being the tonic and doh in both major and minor. The third note of the minor scale is flatter than the third note of the major scale, me becoming maw. The sol-fa names therefore correspond to the mental effects already linked up with sol-fa names in the major scale: leading note tonic is te doh' in both modes. So it is therefore thought of *aurally*, but does not correspond visually to the notation of the minor scale.

Here is C harmonic minor, with its key signature in both soh–fa notations:

Whatever method the teacher adopts for teaching the minor scale: C minor or A minor first; tonic before relative minor; harmonic before melodic, or vice versa, it is fraught with difficulties, because the notation is so confusing.

The teacher who has never used either method of sol-fa names should weigh up the points on each side. The teacher who has been brought up with one method should try to forget it and think the question out afresh. The instrumental teacher should realise that the class teacher may be using a different method and thereby causing confusion; and the two should consult each other, if possible.

However, if one thinks primarily of the aural effect, and of aural training, the doh minor method is the better. Certainly, pupils who have been brought up on it or who have changed to it show less confusion than the others. Its advantages grow as pupils begin to study harmony. For example, I, IV and V are the doh, fah and soh chords in both modes, the dominant seventh is soh te ray fah in both, and so on, the sol-fa names consistently applying to the same effect. (But if, in an advanced examination, a dictation test is given in one of the older modes such as aeolian or dorian there may be a case for calling the tonic lah or ray.)

The minor mode is taught some time after the major mode by most teachers; and by this time pupils should be able to pass through the various stages of ear training more quickly, and should be more familiar with notation.

The following exercises go through the same stages as the major scale exercises but move more quickly; and the exercises use keys up to three sharps and flats. Some teachers will start with C minor, while others start with A minor. The exercises can have their keys changed or be otherwise adapted to fit in with the teacher's methods.

(a) Any one note

The teacher can easily make up his own tests for this, but he may be glad of guidance as to order. The tonic should be played before each note is given.

(b) Three to five notes

The tonic chord (minor key in each case) should be played before each test.

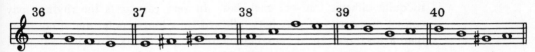

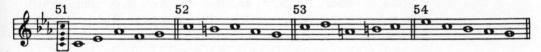

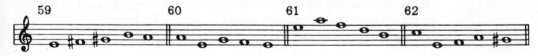

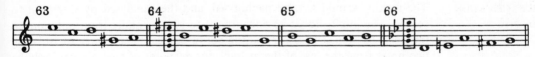

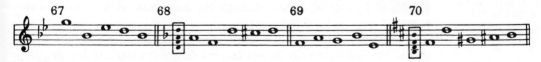

Section IV
Melody

REPRODUCTION Reproduction requirements vary from reproducing a phrase of a few notes to quite difficult four-bar melodies. In very easy tests the rhythm may consist of a series of crotchets followed by a longer note; and if not more than a few notes are required, some of the pitch tests given in Section III may be used, playing them in the rhythm required for a particular examination. Some of the easiest tests given in this Section contain no more than seven notes; and many consist of crotchets followed by a longer note, therefore being suitable for the easier examinations. Many other tests in this Section have no note shorter than a quaver; and a large proportion of them are in keys C, G and F major, as these are common requirements in the easier examinations.

But tests that require nothing more than reproduction may contain more difficult intervals and be in more difficult keys than those in which the pupil is asked to identify the pitch; and they may have more difficult rhythms than those which are required for written dictation. The teacher should therefore be able to find exercises for reproduction purposes in all the first five parts of this Section. Those in parts 6 and 7 could also be used, if they were dictated in sections.

In more difficult reproduction tests it is usually found that the middle section of the test is the part that has been forgotten. Tests should gradually get longer until the pupil can remember quite long phrases. He should be encouraged to sing the **phrase** mentally before he sings it aloud. If the test is played more than once, time should be allowed for mental singing between each playing of the test.

IDENTIFICATION OF PITCH

The melody should first be memorised, and then analysed by singing it to sol-fa. The pupil should be encouraged to sing mentally from one note to the next, by step if necessary, using sol-fa names. The power of isolating two notes from the rest of the melody, for purposes of analysis, can only be developed by mental singing, though the pupil may, at first, have to sing aloud.

If he is required to give the letter names of the notes in a certain key he should think of these *after* he has decided the sol-fa names, translating from sol-fa to letter names.

The tests which follow in this Section are carefully graded; and pupils will gain in confidence by working through these stages, whether they are required for an examination or not. But they do also fit with various examination requirements. Any tests in parts 1–7 may be given for identification purposes, varying from grade I to diploma standard, those in parts 6 and 7 being given in sections.

In some of the easiest written melodic dictation examination tests the note values of all the notes are given. The teacher can easily do this with the easier tests given in this Section, if he wishes. In others the time signature is given. In others the test starts on the first note of the bar. The teacher can easily leave out the anacrusis in any anacrusic tests given below, if he wishes, and lengthen the last note to correspond.

Some examinations state that their melodic dictation tests will start on doh, while others give the first note.

But, whether required for an examination or not, these are useful preliminary stages, leading to the writing down of a complete melody.

The exercises given in this Section follow useful stages which can lead to the writing down of more difficult melodies.

Most pupils find writing down the pitch of a melody more difficult than writing down its rhythm; therefore they should deal with the pitch before the rhythm. An additional reason for doing this is that the rhythm is usually simpler in a melody test than in one in which the rhythm only has to be written.

As stated in writing from dictation in Section III the most important thing is starting on the right note of the scale. Many an examination candidate has written a dictated melody wrongly throughout because he has started on the wrong note. It is for this reason that some of the easiest examinations give doh as the first note; and many of the easiest tests given below do start on doh.

The next most common note to start on is soh, and this particularly applies to melodies with an anacrusic rhythm. If the melody starts on the first beat of the bar, me is a common first note. Both me and soh are easy to recognise as first notes; and the easiest examples in this Section start on doh, me or soh.

But unless the pupil is told the first note, he should mentally sing doh when it is first played and sing up or down to the first note in sol-fa as soon as he hears it, writing down its name over the staff straight away. It does not matter if he has very little idea of the rest of the melody at the first hearing: the first note is the most important thing he must know—and he will probably need continual reminders of this fact.

Suppose the following has to be written:

After the first hearing the pupil may have no more than:

m   d

At the second hearing he should memorise as much of the melody as possible, then analyse it mentally to sol-fa, from one note to the next, and write down the sol-fa names over the staff. He may not have memorised the complete melody at this hearing, but he should write down as much as he can in sol-fa and then wait for the next hearing to memorise the rest.

Memorisation comes before analysis; and for this reason the pupil should listen keenly to the melody as a whole (after having decided the first note), each time it is played, and try to sing it mentally and capture it in his mind before proceeding with detailed analysis. The pupil who listens to a particular interval which is causing difficulty, ignoring the rest of the melody, is wasting his opportunities.

After the second hearing of the above melody he may perhaps have:

m   s   d   f   m r   l₁   t₁   d

Fah, the fourth note, may have caused difficulty. The pupil should sing by step from the third to the fourth note, doh to fah.

While he is waiting for the third hearing he can write small dots on the correct lines and spaces, thus:

m   s   d   f   m r   l₁   t₁   d

At the third hearing he can probably listen for the accents, putting in the bar lines as it is played, and also memorise the tune as a whole, so that he can isolate the missing notes and add them. He will then have this:

m   s   d   f   m r   l   s   l₁   t₁   d

It is much better to put in the bar lines (a bar line is a thing you *hear*) before adding the note lengths. Pupils so often put in the note lengths first and then add the bar lines afterwards, mathematically, without listening for the accents. For example, in the following melody, quite a proportion of examination candidates will write  instead of and produce:

After the third hearing there is a good chance that the pupil can complete the melody without hearing it again, making the little dots larger for black notes and turning them into the edge of a white note. He should add the time signature last. If the melody is played a fourth time he can then check from his complete version.

It is recommended that for some considerable time the pupil should follow the order suggested above, i.e. (*a*) sol-fa name of the first note; (*b*) as much as possible of the rest of the tune to sol-fa; (*c*) tiny dots under the sol-fa names on the right lines and spaces in the particular key; (*d*) bar lines; (*e*) note lengths; (*f*) time signature.

But he should not waste his time between hearings: he should put down as much as he can each time. It is possible, for example, that he has recognised ♩.♩♩ in the above melody before he is sure of the pitch; and in that case he can write this pattern in short hand or note values above the staff.

As the pupil becomes more proficient he should be able to think the sol-fa names and realise the fixed pitch names of the notes in the key at the same time, so that he can write the notes on the staff straight away, without needing to write the sol-fa names at all. But the pupil who always thinks the melody in sol-fa, even when it is quite difficult, and perhaps includes modulation, is the one who makes few or no mistakes in melodic dictation.

One G.C.E. O Level examination gives the melody for dictation first with and then without its harmonic background. The teacher can add a few harmonies to the melodies given below if this is required. The melodies in Section IX could also be used, though they are not so well adapted and graded for this purpose as are those in this Section.

Another G.C.E. O Level examination gives two melodies for dictation, the second of which may be a variation of the first. The teacher can make up his own variants of the melodies given below, for this purpose.

1 Two-, Three- and Four-Bar melodies in easy major keys; $\frac{2}{4}$, $\frac{3}{4}$ or $\frac{4}{4}$ time; no note shorter than a crotchet

(*a*) *Melody lying between doh and soh, and starting on doh. Keys C, G and F major*

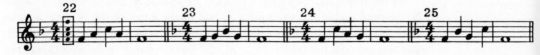

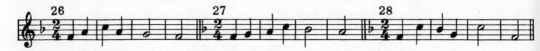

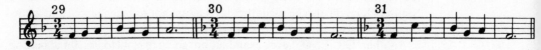

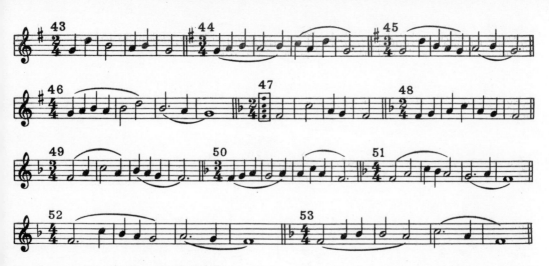

(b) Pentatonic scale; keys C, G and F

Some teaching methods make use of the pentatonic scale, and some examinations require it in early stages. The pupils should be told that only the notes of the pentatonic scale will be used. Teachers who do not make use of the pentatonic scale as a stage in their teaching should go straight on to (c), which most pupils will find easier.

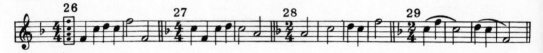

(c) Complete major scale, but the only leaps are between notes of the tonic chord

Teachers who do not use the pentatonic scale as a stage in their teaching will go straight from the tests in (a) to those below.

Leaps between notes of the tonic chord are more common than other leaps and, if the pupil has established the tonic chord as a tonal basis in his mind, he will find the tonic chord leaps easy to recognise.

Some C.S.E. examinations confine their dictation tests to the kind given below.

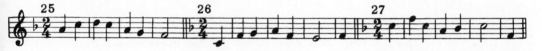

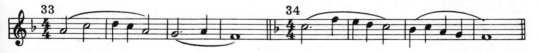

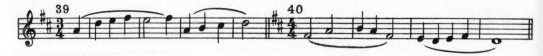

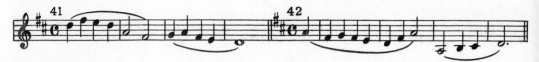

(d) *As for* (c), *but also including any leap of a third*

This is slightly more difficult than (c), but is again a C.S.E. type of test.

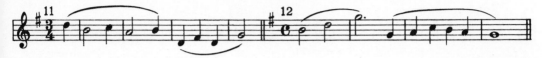

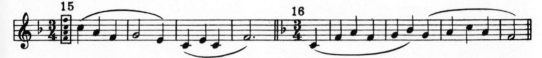

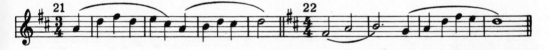

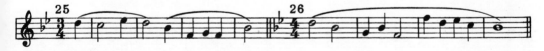

2 The introduction of quavers and easy leaps, in easy major keys

(*a*) *Two- and three-bar phrases*

This kind of melody might be given for reproduction in practical examinations about grade IV or V. It is also suitable for easy dictation tests. The tests in major keys given in Section II, part 1 (*a*) (*b*) and (*c*), may also be used for melodic dictation.

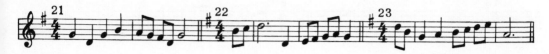

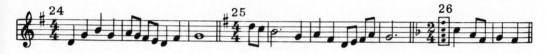

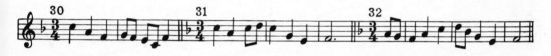

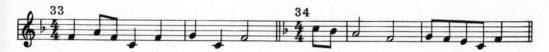

(b) *Four-bar phrases*

Melodies for dictation are rarely less than four bars long. But they are frequently dictated in halves. Some C.S.E. tests are about this standard. The tests in a major key in Section II, part 1 (*d*) may also be used for this purpose.

58

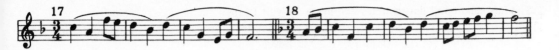

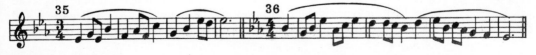

3 The introduction of dotted notes and more difficult Leaps

The melodies in this part are all four bars long, and are of the kind often given for dictation in G.C.E. O Level.

Teachers who want shorter passages for reproduction purposes can give half of any of these tests, divided according to the phrase marks.

The tests given in major keys in Section II, parts 2 and 4 (*a*) may also be used for this purpose.

4 Easy four-bar melodies in ⅝ time, easy major keys

At first pupils may be told when a melody is in compound time. Later they must decide for themselves (see the comments in Section II, part 3).

Examples of two-bar and three-bar phrases in compound time which can be used for reproduction purposes will be found in Section II parts 3 and 5 (*a*). The four-bar examples may also be used as additional to those given here.

This is the type of melody that might be given as a dictation test in G.C.E. O Level.

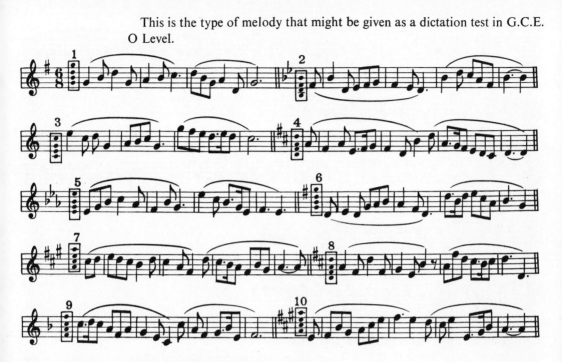

5 Easy four-bar melodies in easy minor keys

The pupil should first work the pitch tests without rhythm in easy minor keys in Section III, part 7. He can then go on to sing or write, as melodies, any exercises given in the minor key in Section II, starting with those which are only two or three bars long. The four-bar melodies given here are the kind that might be given for dictation in G.C.E. O Level, and are graded in order of difficulty.

6 More-difficult four-bar melodies in any major key

Some G.C.E. A Level examinations give melodies which are complex rather than long, while others give longer melodies containing chromatic notes and modulation, but which are relatively straightforward. The following exercises are suitable for the former type of examination.

7 More-difficult four-bar melodies in any minor key

These are again the type of melody that might be given in some G.C.E. A Level examinations.

8 Five- to eight-bar diatonic melodies

Longer melodies must always be dictated in sections. Most Examining Boards state how often a melody will be repeated, and how it will be divided into sections. But the teacher must make his intentions clear to the pupil; and the pupil must be particularly careful about the joins.

The examples given in this part contain no chromatic notes and do not modulate, so the pupil should find it relatively easy to keep the tonic in his head throughout and, in particular, to relate the first note of each new phrase to the tonic. He should be particularly careful about the interval between the last note of one phrase and the first note of the next.

All pupils should work a few exercises of this type before going on to those containing chromatic notes or modulation. Longer melodies, however, are more likely to modulate.

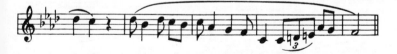

9 Five- to eight-bar melodies containing chromatic notes

The chromatic notes in these melodies are purely decorative, and do not change the key. The pupil should think in sol-fa. It is presumed that he knows about the notation of the melodic chromatic scale. The decorative note invariably has a different letter name from the note it decorates. For example, it is wrong to write any flats in example 1; and the double sharps are necessary in example 3. This pre-supposes, on the part of the pupil, either a knowledge of, or an instinctive realisation of which is the harmony note and which is the decorative one.

10 Eight-bar melodies containing modulations

The first stage is to recognise the aural effect of various modulations. Therefore parts of Section X should be studied before students learn to *write* melodies containing modulations from dictation. The effect of modulation should be pointed out in any songs or other music the student happens to study.

He should then learn how to modulate, and should have some knowledge of common key schemes before writing down modulating melodies from dictation. The first examples here contain just one modulation, to the dominant from a major key, or to the relative major from a minor key, the most common modulations, which the student should learn to compose first. The later examples contain more than one modulation, but they occur to keys and in places which are natural, and the student should be able to compose similar melodies himself.

Knowing where modulations are likely to occur, and the keys to which they are likely to go, provides a useful check on what a student has written from dictation. He should be familiar with the kind of modulating sequences that occur in the later examples. He should never lose the feel of the key centre, though he should think of the sol-fa names of the new key for each modulation.

Some G.C.E. A Level examinations give this kind of melody for dictation; and they might occur as dictation tests in class music diplomas.

11 Nine- to twelve-bar melodies containing modulations

Some G.C.E. A Level examinations set a melody of up to twelve bars long for dictation. With longer melodies it is even more important that the student never loses hold of the tonal centre, and that he can relate each modulation to that key centre, and also to the keys that precede and follow it.

Section V
Intervals

1 Reproduction of upper and lower notes of an interval, played harmonically

Singing the top note of an interval is little more difficult than singing a note which is heard by itself. But many people find difficulty in distinguishing the lower of two sounds.

If, for example [♪] is heard, they may unconsciously hear the effect as a chord and sing G, which is part of the chord but not actually present.

The pupil should be taught to listen intently and not to attempt to sing the lower note until he is sure he has really heard it. He should mentally sing the top note first, then dismiss it from his mind and listen intently until the bottom note begins to stand out. A good analogy is that of leaving a brightly-lit house in the country on a dark night. At first one can see nothing. But if one stands and waits, after a moment the path begins to loom up out of the darkness. In the same way, the bottom note will begin to 'loom up', to differentiate itself from the one above; and the pupil should wait patiently until it does so. In some strange way, it even appears to grow louder (providing that the teacher continues to hold the notes down).

If necessary, the teacher may play the bottom note a little louder than the top one, in the earliest stages.

It should be obvious that, whether this is an examination requirement or not, it is an essential preliminary to naming an interval or a chord, or recognising a tune in a lower or middle part, an ability which is essential to the real enjoyment of all but the very simplest music; and all pupils should be given practice in hearing and reproducing a note with a higher note above it. But many Examining Boards do, in fact, require this in their easier examinations.

(a) Consonant intervals only (third, fifth, sixth and octave)

Most pupils find this easier than singing the lower note of a discord; and some examinations give it as a first requirement.

The teacher can easily make up these tests for himself; but a few are given here as examples of the kind required. Examples in part 2 (*a*) can also be used.

(b) Consonant and dissonant intervals

Notes which are close together are usually more difficult to differentiate than those which are further apart.

A few examples are given here, to which the teacher can add more. Any other intervals given in this Section can also be used.

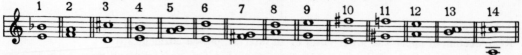

2 Recognition of the size of an interval (number only), heard melodically or harmonically

This is the next stage. When the pupil has learnt to hear both notes of an interval he can sing upwards from the lower one to the higher one, counting as he does so. He may sing aloud at first, but eventually he should be able to do this mentally. At this stage he is required to give the number of the interval only, without reference to its quality.

It is obvious that it is easier for the pupil if the notes are played one after the other (melodically), rather than harmonically. So they should be given melodically before they are heard harmonically. They are written harmonically in the examples which follow, but the teacher can play them either way.

(a) Consonant intervals only (third, fifth, sixth and octave)

If the pupil knows that the intervals are limited to the third, fifth, sixth and octave he should have little difficulty in recognising the third and the octave. The fifth and sixth are more difficult, as they are closer together in size. In addition to counting, the pupil should listen to the general effect. The consonant fifth (the perfect fifth) is bare in sound; and it is often useful to link it with the sound of the tuning of violins. The consonant sixth (major or minor) is softer and less bare.

It may be wise for the teacher to give a number of fifths and sixths after each other, for the purposes of comparison.

In addition to the examples given here the teacher may also use those given in part 1 (*a*). But he can easily make up as many more as are required.

(b) Consonant and dissonant intervals, omitting the tritone

If a pupil is asked to name the number of an interval in isolation, that is, without reference to a key, it is obvious that there must be no doubt about its size. For this reason the tritone cannot be used: a fifth, may equally will be heard as a fourth. However, if heard in isolation, would instinctively be heard as a sixth, rather than an augmented fifth; and [music: staff with note] would be heard as a sixth, rather than

[music: staff with note] a diminished seventh.

In effect, therefore, the intervals available for this purpose are major and minor seconds, thirds, sixths and sevenths, and perfect fourths, fifths and octaves. The pupil will not, however, at this stage, use the words major, minor or perfect.

He should continue to sing up from the bottom note to the top one, counting as he does so.

But, in addition, he can ask himself whether the interval is small, medium or large. If it is small, it will either be the discordant second or the concordant third; if large, it will either be the concordant sixth or the discordant seventh. He will probably find the greatest difficulty with the fourth and the fifth. He should realise that the fifth, though bare, is concordant and does not require a resolution, whereas a fourth, heard in isolation is discordant and

wants to resolve: [music: staff] It will help him if he thinks of a fourth as doh fah, and mentally resolves it on to doh me, as above; while he should think of the fifth as doh soh.

The examples given below are carefully graded, and give practice in comparisons. The pupil can, at first, be told that the interval is a second or third; a sixth or seventh, or a fourth or fifth. Then the intervals should be mixed. At this stage, a further reminder may be necessary that the pupil should *listen* for the bottom note, rather than make it up. He may, for example, confuse a sixth with a third, because the harmonic effect is similar.

seconds and thirds

sixths and sevenths

fourths and fifths

mixed

The exercises in part 1 (*b*), omitting numbers 1 and 11 may be used next. The teacher can then make up as many more tests as he needs.

(c) Any diatonic interval from the tonic of a major key

Some examinations, including those of some C.S.E. Boards, ask for the recognition of any major or perfect interval. This, in effect, means that the pupil has to think of the lower note as the tonic of a major key, and then to recognise the interval by number only, as in *(a)* and *(b)* above. It will be major if it is the second, third, sixth or seventh of the scale, or perfect if it is the fourth, fifth or octave; and the reason for this can easily be explained to the pupil.

He is not being asked to differentiate aurally between major and minor, or between perfect, augmented and diminished: the interval is automatically major or perfect if it is between the tonic and an upper note of the scale. So the test more properly comes under the heading of part 2 of this Section than of part 3.

Test *(c)* therefore involves the recognition of the concords heard in *(a)* plus the perfect fourth, the major second and the major seventh heard in *(b)*. But fewer intervals are involved than in *(b)*, because no minor intervals will be given. However, within this narrow field, the pupil is asked to state the number and the quality of the interval. The pupil recognises the interval by counting, as in *(a)* and *(b)* above. But he will get to know the sound of these intervals better if he always calls the lower note doh, and sings up to the upper note using sol-fa names.

Some examples of this kind are given here; but the teacher can easily make up more by playing a tonic and any note of the major scale above it.

(d) Any interval of a major key, given the tonic

This is occasionally given as a test. It can follow on from either *(b)* or *(c)*. But as the tonic is *not* necessarily the lowest note of the interval, the pupil is not expected to state the quality of the interval at this stage. He will, however, think in sol-fa, having been given the tonic, and this will act as a check to the counting method suggested in *(a)* and *(b)*.

The only additional interval that may occur in *(d)* below, as compared with *(b)* above, is the tritone, which occurs between fah and te in a major key. Given C as tonic, it can be given as a fourth: or as a fifth: ; and the pupil should be able to state which it is.

The tonic should be played each time before every interval given below. Examples are given with C, G and F as tonic, but the teacher can make up similar examples with any note as the tonic. As the pupil has only to state the number of the interval, without referring to its quality or naming its notes, one key is, however, no more difficult than another.

3 Recognition of the size of an interval (number and quality) heard melodically or harmonically, without relation to a key note

Even though an interval is given for recognition without a preliminary key note, anyone naturally hears an interval diatonically and, in practice, as it would occur in a major key. For example: would be heard as a minor seventh; would be heard as a minor sixth; and would be heard as a major third.

So the intervals available are the same as those which have been given under 2 (d), even though the pupil is not given a key note. But now he has to state the quality as well as the size of the interval.

The modification of intervals can be learnt from a theory book. But, when it comes to aural recognition, they can best be learnt in the stages shown below. They can first be given melodically, if the teacher wishes; and when they are given harmonically the teacher may play the bottom note a little louder in the first stages.

(a) Major and minor third

The pupil should think of the bottom note as doh and then sing, aloud or mentally, the arpeggio of the major chord and the arpeggio of the minor chord, in order to see to which chord the interval belongs. He should use sol-fa names.

(b) Major and minor sixth

There are two ways of differentiating between these two intervals. The teacher can suggest that his pupils use either method, but they should always use the *same* method, otherwise confusion can easily be caused.

The pupil with a strong sense of tonality will probably hear 🎼 as an incomplete tonic chord of a major key (C major), and therefore as me doh'. This is good, and natural, as long as he realises that it is an inversion of a major third of the major tonic chord: 🎼 and is therefore a *minor* sixth, even though it has a feeling of a major key. If the pupil sings up the major arpeggio, as suggested in dealing with thirds, he will realise it is part of this major chord.

Alternatively the pupil may be taught to think of the bottom note as doh. Hearing 🎼 he will therefore sing, aloud or mentally, 🎼 in E major, and then realise that the note he has heard in a semitone below the sixth note of the scale, and is therefore a minor sixth.

Similarly 🎼 can be thought of as an incomplete tonic chord of a minor key (C minor), and therefore a *major* sixth, or as the major sixth of the major scale starting with the bottom note as doh (E flat).

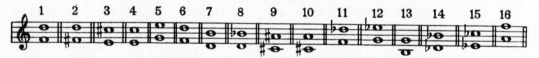

As some pupils manage to confuse thirds and sixths, the next stage is to mix examples from 3 (a) and 3 (b), asking the pupil to state the size and the quality of the interval.

(c) Major and minor second

It is easy to differentiate between these two intervals because the minor second, the semitone, is so much more discordant than the major second, the tone.

Two further devices are helpful. One is to associate the tone with doh ray, and the semitone with te, doh. The other is to try to sing another sound between the two notes. If this can be done the interval is a major second.

Now is the moment to give a mixture of major and minor seconds, and major and minor thirds, and ask for a full description. Examples can be taken from (a) and (c) in this part.

(d) Major and minor seventh

The relative dissonance of sevenths is the opposite of that of seconds, the major seventh being the more discordant of the two. This is because it is the inversion of the minor second, the semitone, which two notes are closer together.

The major seventh can be thought of as doh te; while the minor seventh will, to many students, make them think of the dominant seventh, reminding them of , which they may have learnt to play as a piano arpeggio, or to use in their harmony exercises. In other words, they will think of the outside notes as being soh and fah.

The pupil can now be asked to name any major or minor second, third, sixth or seventh. Tests can be picked out at random from those given above.

(e) Perfect fourth, perfect fifth and tritone

The pupil has already learnt to recognise the perfect fourth and fifth under 2 (*b*) and (*c*). He should think of the perfect fourth as doh fah, and the perfect fifth as doh soh.

The tritone, played without relation to a key note, may be heard as an augmented fourth, fah te: , wanting to resolve outwards, or as diminished fifth, te fah: , wanting to resolve inwards.

Obviously both answers are correct. But another possible answer is to call the interval a tritone. This should be accepted by any examiner, and it evades the issue of augmented fourth versus diminished fifth, which depends upon a purely subjective feeling, if no tonic is given.

The perfect fifth, though bare, is a concord. The perfect fourth, heard without any other sound, is a discord requiring resolution. But it has nothng like as strong a feeling of movement as has the tritone.

The tritone is, however, quite often mistaken for the minor seventh, and both giving the effect of an incomplete dominant seventh. But if the pupil counts, as he sings up from the bottom note to the top one, he should not fall into this error.

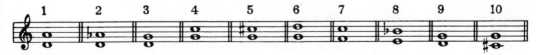

(f) Any interval within an octave

The pupil should now be in a position to recognise the number and quality of any interval within an octave.

He should consider the interval in three stages: (1) large, medium or small; (2) consonant or dissonant; (3) quality.

Some examples are given here, making use of comparisons between similar intervals in juxtaposition. After this the teacher can use any of the intervals given in this Section, at random.

This test is a requirement in a number of G.C.E. O Level examinations.

4 Naming and writing down the notes of an interval, given the key

This test asks the student to relate the sounds of an interval to a given key, and to be able to name the notes or write them down in that key. It is required in some G.C.E. A Level examinations.

The student should hear each note in sol-fa, in relation to the key and write it down. He should then name the resultant interval, using his theoretical knowledge, and finally check to see if his naming corresponds with the expected aural effect.

(a) Diatonic in a major key

It is helpful to realise that the only dimished or augmented intervals in a major key are formed by the tritone, fah te, producing either an augmented fourth or a diminished fifth: in key C major.

But now the student must differentiate between the two, because the key is given: the tritone is no longer a sufficient answer.

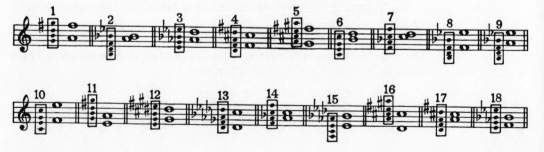

78

(b) Diatonic in a minor key

A list of the possible diminished and augmented intervals in the harmonic form of the minor scale may be helpful. In C minor they are:

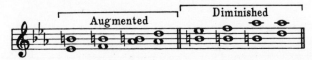

Intervals which involve notes peculiar to the melodic minor scale are less likely to be given in an interval test, because they would only occur in a melodic progression of several notes. A few are included here, though the place for their recognition is really in a progression as in Section VI.

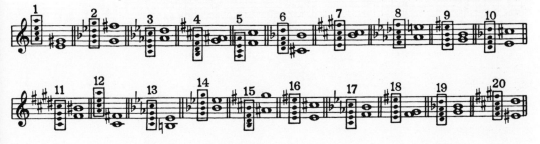

(c) Intervals which are formed by chromatic notes in a major or minor key

There are a few intervals which can only occur in a chromatic scale. They are the augmented first: ♩ and its inversion, the diminished octave ♩ ; and the augmented sixth: ♩ and its inversion, the diminished third: ♩

The augmented sixth can occur on the minor second (raw) and the minor sixth (law) of the scale: D flat and A flat in C major or C minor. Its inversion, the diminished third, is very rarely found.

Other intervals involving chromatic notes might occur in any major or minor key. For example, ♩ which is diatonic in key G might occur in key C.

Chromatic intervals would only be given in the most advanced kind of aural tests; and it would be much more reasonable to give them in a progression, as in Section VI. But a few are given here, in isolation. The tonic chord of the major or minor key should be stated and played before each interval.

Major keys

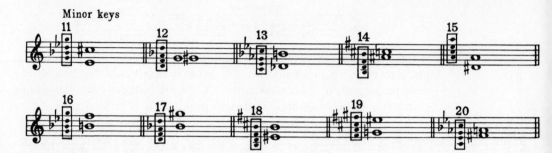

Section VI
Two-Part Tests

REPRODUCTION
OF EITHER PART
Quite a number of the higher practical examinations require the reproduction, either by singing or playing, of the upper or the lower part of a short two-part passage.

The upper part presents no difficulties if the two parts have the same note lengths, as in part 1 below.

But if the two parts are rhythmically different, and particularly if one part starts with an imitation of the other, the student may find a little difficulty in disentangling the two parts.

The teacher may help, in the first stages, by playing the two parts with a different tone colour, and particularly by playing the part that has to be reproduced rather more loudly.

The student should listen for the long notes so that he can tell, for example, that in the following passage the E is held on and the G and C are therefore in the lower part:

He should be able to recognise imitative entries and realise, for example, that in the following passage the upper part starts on C D F with an imitation of the lower C F A:

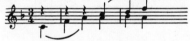

If he has composed in two parts himself he is more likely to realise how the parts fit, to make musical sense.

Reproduction of the lower part is always more difficult. Preliminary work should have been done in listening for the lower note of an interval in isolation in Section V; and the analogy, given in that Section, between waiting for a lower part to 'loom up' and waiting for a path to 'loom up' on a dark night, still applies. The student should gradually learn how to hear a lower part as a melody. Listening to tunes played by lower instruments in an orchestral work, or to the lower part of a two-part song are both helpful aids to improvement; and following a lower part from a score while a work is sung or played will facilitate its aural recognition.

WRITING BOTH
PARTS FROM
DICTATION
The best way of doing this is to try to hear both parts as separate tunes, and to write them down using the methods recommended in Section IV.

They should then be studied to see if they make musical sense, and to check that the intervals produced do sound like themselves: for example, that a sixth sounds like a sixth, a seventh like a seventh, and so on.

D

Short phrases, particularly if the lower part is required to be reproduced, are usually written as treble and alto parts on the treble stave.

But, if the two parts are meant to be written down, some examinations give one part on the treble stave and the other on the bass. Some students find the parts easier to distinguish if they are further apart.

Many people, however, find it easier to hear a part which is within the range of their own voice. For this reason, men often find it easier to hear a bass than do women and children.

The easiest examples given here always have the two parts on the treble stave. Later ones have some on one stave, some in two. But the teacher can easily change most of them by playing the lower part an octave higher or an octave lower, as the case may be. If a student finds difficulty one way the teacher should experiment by trying the other.

Hearing a part in the treble and a part in the bass is a useful preliminary to recognising the bass line of s chord ear test.

1 A series of three to six intervals

This is a requirement in some G.C.E. O Level dictation tests. Reproduction tests for practical examinations more often make use of contrasted rhythms, as in part 2 below.

(*a*) *Major keys*

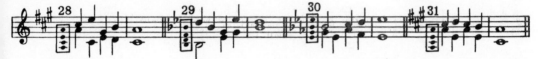

(b) Minor keys

2 A two- or three-bar phrase in two parts

This is the kind of test that is often given for reproduction in practical examinations.

But these tests can also be given for dictation, and act as a useful preparation for the longer tests in parts 3 and 4. If one part starts before the other, the student must not forget to insert the appropriate rests.

(a) Major keys

(b) Minor keys

3 A four-bar passage in two parts

This is the kind of test that might be given for dictation at G.C.E. A Level, though some Boards give longer tests than these. It is also given in one practical diploma examination.

These tests should be dictated in sections. Some Boards state how they are to be divided and how often they are to be given. It is usual to play the passage straight through at the beginning and the end, so the student should be in no doubt as to how the sections join. He should be particularly careful that the intervals are correct at the join.

The student should analyse the harmonic implications of the passage, to be sure he has written musical sense.

If one part starts before the other it is often best to write this part first, in its entirety.

The student should not spend too long in attending to either part at the expense of the other. He will not get very high marks if the top part is quite correct and the bottom has not been written at all.

The points made in Section IV about the importance of starting on the right note and of memorising as much as possible of the tune, thinking it in sol-fa before writing it down, still apply, of course, to this Section. But now the student has two tunes to memorise; and he must learn to hear the lower part as a tune.

When a passage starts with imitative entries some students forget to add rests to the silent part. In other cases they are careless about the notation of the rests, forgetting, for example, that a whole bar's silence requires a semibreve rest, even in duple or triple time.

(a) Two parts on the treble stave

89

4 A five- or six-bar passage in two parts

These passages are intended for dictation. Some G.C.E. A Level tests are of this standard, as are also dictation tests for class music diplomas.

(*a*) *Two parts on the treble stave*

(b) One part on the treble stave and the other on the bass

Section VII
Single Chord Tests

VARIOUS
EXAMINATION
REQUIREMENTS

Most C.S.E. Examination Boards do not give any kind of chord test. But one Board asks for the recognition of the recurrence of three harmonies, which comes under the heading of Section VIII, while another Board asks for the recognition of the number of notes in a chord, up to four, which is covered in part 3 below. A few Boards ask for the recognition of cadences, which comes under Section IX.

All the Practical Examination Boards ask for the recognition of a particular chord in isolation, in their higher grades and practical diploma examinations. In nearly all cases it is a triad, in root position or inversion, in close or open position, and is therefore covered in part 4 below.

One practical diploma examination requires the candidates to hum or play the middle or bottom note of any three-part chord, which is covered in parts 1 and 2 below. Another diploma examination asks for the recognition of the dominant seventh and its inversions in addition to triads, and this is covered in part 5 below. These chords may also have to be written after one note has been named.

One higher grade practical examination asks for the recognition of one of the three primary triads, in its root position or inverted, after the tonic chord has been played. But this is the only practical examination which asks for the recognition of a chord in relation to a key; and, even in this case, only one chord has to be recognised, not a chord progression. This is covered in part 7 below.

Only one O Level examination asks for the recognition of a single chord in isolation. A major chord is played in four parts, and the candidate has to say if it is in its root position, first or second inversion. This is covered in part 6 below.

Most O Level and all A Level examinations ask for the recognition of a progression of chords in relation to a key. This is covered in Section VIII, and is a different kind of test from the single chords given in Section VII.

The teacher who is preparing a pupil for a practical examination must therefore work some or all of Section VII; and the tests are given in logical order, one part leading to the next.

But the teacher who is preparing a pupil for a G.C.E. O Level or A Level examination does not need to work through Section VII as a preliminary to Section VIII. He will encourage his pupils to hear chords in relation to a key from the beginning, and will be more concerned with the recognition of the general effect of the chord and the identification of its bass note than with the arrangement of three particular notes making some form of triad.

The teacher who is not preparing a pupil for an examination can choose whether to use Section VII or Section VIII or both. But recognising a chord progression in a key, such as I V I, is of more musical value than recognising a particular arrangement of an isolated triad, such as the rarely used augmented triad.

1 Singing top, middle or bottom notes of a three-note concord

This test is concerned with the ability to hear and differentiate the three notes of a concord, and not with the ability to name the chord. It is a useful preliminary to part 4. The pupil should listen keenly, being sure he has really heard all three notes and not imagined another note which might be part of the chord. Then he should sing slowly and carefully, aloud in the earliest stages, mentally at later stages, all three notes from the top down to the bottom note, before reproducing the particular note that is required.

2 Singing top, middle or bottom notes of a three-note discord

As the three notes become more discordant, so do they become more difficult to differentiate. The following tests are arranged roughly in order of difficulty. Teachers may give the easiest ones only, or even leave out part 2 altogether, if it is not required for examination purposes. The harder tests given below are diploma level; or they might be given in a scholarship or college entrance test.

3 Stating the number of notes in a chord of two, three or four notes

This is again a question of the ability to hear individual notes rather than of recognising a particular kind of chord, though it will act as a useful preliminary to the latter. It is not a regular feature of examinations, but may be set occasionally.

The pupil can only state the number of notes in a chord with confidence if he is able to hear and mentally reproduce all the notes which are present. So, although he is not expected to sing any particular note, the method of working is the same as in parts 1 and 2 above.

The tests below are again graded roughly in order of difficulty. Comparisons can often be made between similar chords; and such chords are bracketed together in the tests which follow.

4 Recognition of isolated triads in close and open position; singing any note; Identification of the top note

All Practical Examination Boards ask for the recognition of triads in close position; and most of them follow the order of identification given below, though some do not deal with the inversions of the common chords before introducing diminished and augmented triads. The teacher who is preparing his pupils for a particular examination can omit or adapt some of the tests given below, if necessary. But the order given here is musical and logical, and should be followed, if possible.

All these Boards also ask their candidates to sing or play the top, middle or bottom note, at one grade or another. The examples given below can be used for this purpose. The candidates may also be asked to name the other notes of the triad when one has been given.

Some Boards also give the triads in open (extended) position in their higher examinations; and in this case they may also ask for the identification of the top note as being the root, third or fifth of the triad. Therefore some examples of triads in open position are given in (c) and (e), the stages at which the test may take this form in practical examinations.

(a) Major and minor triads, root position

It is advisable to think of all major and minor triads, heard in isolation, as being tonic chords.

The pupil should sing, slowly and carefully, down the three notes from the top to the bottom, as in part 1 above. He should then think of the lowest note as doh, and carefully sing up the first five notes of the major scale to sol-fa, with this note as tonic. From this he should be able to tell whether he has heard doh me soh, from the scale he has just sung, or whether the third was flatter, therefore being part of the minor scale. To check and compare, he should then sing the first five notes of the minor scale, to sol-fa. If he can sing accurately doh ray me, and doh ray maw, he should be able to hear the difference.

The minor triad often has a sadder feeling than the major, the difference being made more obvious if the two triads are compared on the same notes. But it is rather unsafe to rely upon this for identification: a minor triad played high up, with a bright, *forte* tone can sound quite cheerful, while a low major triad, played softly, may sound sad.

The piano pupil who is in the habit of playing major and minor arpeggios should have learnt to recognise the difference from his playing, if he keeps his ear alert.

Again, comparisons can be made between the chords bracketed together below. If the pupil makes mistakes in the later tests, the teacher should play the other kind of triad on the same bass note, as a comparison.

(b) Major and minor triads, root position and first inversion

The pupil should first decide whether the triad is in its root position or first inversion. To do this he should sing the notes he has heard from the top to the bottom and decide whether the bottom note is doh. If it is not, he can add another note to the chord, a third below the bass note, so as to reach doh. For example, if he hears [music] he should sing [music] ; if he hears [music] he will similarly sing [music]

If, however, the triad is in its root position he should realise that he has already reached doh when he sings the bottom note. But it is always possible to continue singing down the arpeggio; so, hearing [music] he may sing [music], not realising that F is doh and not C. But he should avoid this error, if his sense of tonality has been well trained, and sol-fa names are really linked to their aural effect in his mind. It is as well, however, to point out this possible mistake.

A root position sounds stronger and more finished than a first inversion, because of the presence of the root in the bass. The pupil should realise that it is the bass note which is the deciding factor, not the top note.

Another means of deciding between a first inversion and a root position, which can be used to check the answer obtained by the means described above, is to sing by step from one note of the chord down to the next, so as to discover the intervals the chord contains. A root position consist of two thirds:

[music]

whereas a first inversion has a fourth between its upper notes:

[music]

Having decided whether the triad is in root position or inverted, the pupil must now decide whether it is major or minor; and he should do this as suggested in (a) above. The chord consists of doh me soh or doh maw soh, however it is arranged; and if the pupil sings the complete arpeggio from doh up to doh', he should be able to tell whether he is singing a major or a minor chord. If he makes a mistake, it should be sufficient for the teacher to play the alternative chord—major instead of minor, or vice versa—for him to realise his error.

In tests 1–16 below some chords are again bracketed together, for purposes of comparison.

(c) Major and minor triads, root position and first and second inversion

Second inversions are quite different from root positions and first inversions because they are discords, instead of concords, and want to resolve. Eg.:

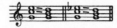

It is the presence of the fourth from the bass note—G to C in the above chords—that makes the discord and requires the resolution.

Although the chords are heard in isolation, that is, without reference to a key, it is still best to think of them as a part of a major or minor tonic chord or arpeggio, doh me soh or doh maw soh. Soh is the bass note in a second inversion.

If the triads are given in close position it is helpful to listen for the presence and position of the interval of a fourth:

There is no fourth in a root position; the fourth is between the two top notes in a first inversion; and between the two bottom notes in a second inversion. Singing and counting from one note down to the next is a useful means of checking the answer.

Similar tests are grouped by a bracket in 1–20 below; and it will be an advantage to give them this way, at first, for purposes of comparison. Later the teacher should give the same tests in random order.

Open (extended) position. Some of the more advanced practical examinations give triads for recognition in the open or extended position. There are still only three notes of the triad, a root, a third and a fifth, but the notes are not adjacent notes of the chord: one of the notes of the chord is left out between each pair of notes.

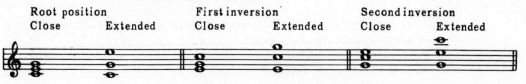

This may mean, in some cases, that the range is too wide for the top or bottom note to be sung. An examiner will only ask for notes to be sung that are within the range of the candidate's voice.

It is obvious that, in an extended-position triad, the suggestions for recognising the position of a triad by locating the presence of the interval of a fourth no longer apply. The pupil must now rely upon his recognition of the bass note: the root, doh, in the root position, producing a strong, finished effect; the third, me or maw, in the first inversion, producing a less finished effect; or the fifth, soh, in the second inversion, producing a discord. It may be helpful to recognise me in the bass by thinking of the first note of 'Three Blind Mice'.

He may also be asked to state which note, root, third or fifth, is at the top, as a choice is now possible.

All the tests given below are in extended position. But, when the teacher is giving the tests to the pupil he should mix them with the tests in close position, given above.

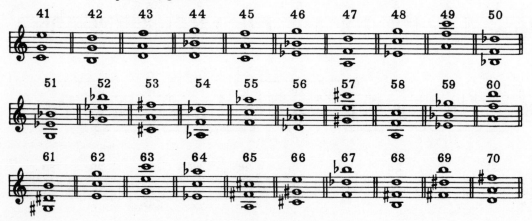

(*d*) *Major, minor, diminished and augmented triads, root position*
Some Examining Boards ask for the recognition of diminished and augmented triads before they ask for the inversion of any kind of triad. Accord-

ingly, this kind of test is given below. It is always given with the notes of the triad in close position.

Major and minor triads are concords and are frequently used. They are therefore frequently called 'common chords'. Major and minor triads, or common chords, take their name from the kind of third they contain. Both have a perfect fifth.

Diminished and augmented triads are discords, and are much less frequently used. They are not, therefore, 'common chords'. They both take their name from the kind of fifth they contain.

A diminished triad contains a minor third and a diminished fifth, which results in two minor thirds, one above the other, a weak effect.

Diminished triads occur on the seventh degree of the major and minor scale (VII), and also on the second degree of the minor scale (II).

The student is recommended to think of a diminished triad as VII, and he should listen for te, ray, fah. The presence of the leading note as the root is usually easy to recognise.

The diminished fifth demands a resolution inwards:

This fact, if combined with listening for te as the root, makes the diminished triad easy to recognise.

An augmented triad contains a major third and an augmented fifth, which results in two major thirds, one above the other, a strident effect.

The augmented triad occurs on the third degree of the minor scale III:

The augmented fifth demands a resolution upwards:

The diminished triad, though a discord, requiring a resolution, is a weak, soft and quite pleasant discord. The augmented triad is much harsher and more discordant, and is unlikely to be confused with any of the other three triads.

The use of sol-fa names, combined with the impression of the general effect, should make the student sure of recognising diminished and augmented triads. But, as a further check, he may, if he wishes, sing up from the bass note to the third (doh ray me or doh ray maw), and again from the third to the fifth (doh ray me or doh ray maw), to decide whether the third is major or minor in each case.

In the first stages of giving this test the teacher may again like to compare the triads which are bracketed together below (1–18).

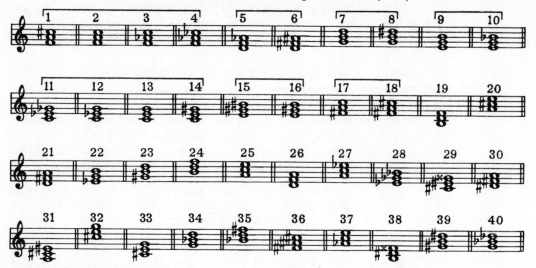

(e) Major, minor and diminished triads in root position and their inversions, and the augmented triad in root position

This test is usually confined to diploma examinations.

The new chord effects, as compared with a combination of (c) and (d) above are concerned solely with the inversions of the diminished triad:

The diminished fifth of the root position, demanding a resolution inwards, becomes an augmented fourth in the first and second inversions, demanding a resolution outwards. But the general impression of soft, discordant weakness is present in all three positions; and they can be identified by the presence of te, ray or fah in the bass.

The augmented triad can be *written* as a root position, a first inversion and a second inversion. But, if heard in isolation, without relation to a key, they all *sound* alike. They all contain two major thirds, one above the other though the notes may be written, enharmonically, as a diminished fourth, This is because a succession of four major thirds produces an octave:

Thus the first inversion of is , which sounds the same as

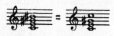, an augmented triad, root position, on E.

The second inversion of the same augmented triad 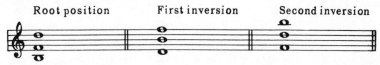 is ..., which sounds the same as ..., an augmented triad, root position, on A♭.

So, if heard in isolation, the only answer to the aural effect of any of the above chords is 'augmented triad'. One cannot state whether it is root position first or second inversion, unless one is given the key.

All these triads may be given for recognition in extended position. The new effects are the diminished triad:

Root position   First inversion   Second inversion

The student should listen for the general impression of the weak, dissonant triad, with te, ray or fah in the bass.

The tests given below consist of a mixture of triads in close and extended position. If, for any particular examination, only triads in close position are required, the teacher can omit the triads in extended position. Otherwise it is desirable to mix them.

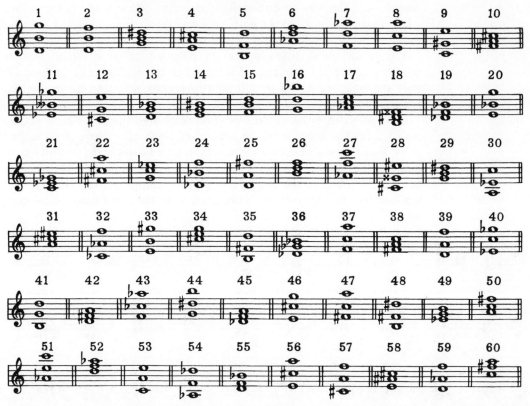

109

5 Recognition of the dominant seventh and its inversions; singing any note; writing down the chord, gives one note

The dominant seventh has four notes and three inversions. It consists of the same notes in a major or minor key on the same tonic.

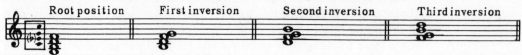

A chord containing a root, third, fifth and seventh can be built on every note of the scale, but that on the dominant is the only one that contains a diminished fifth (or its inversion, the augmented fourth) between its third and seventh notes, te fah, an interval that has already been met with in connection with the diminished triad. And these notes, te fah, resolve in exactly the same way as they do in the diminished triad:

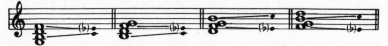

There is a close similarity between the two chords, both being soft, pleasant discords that contain te and fah, and therefore requiring the same resolution. The way to distinguish them is to realise that the diminished triad contains three different notes, whereas the dominant seventh contains four.

The student should listen for the bass note, soh, te ray or fah, in order to tell the position of the chord. It is helpful to realise that te in the bass will have the tendency to rise to doh (first inversion); and that fah in the bass has a tendency to fall (last inversion).

If the chord is given in close position some students may find it helpful to listen for the position of the interval of a second. There is no second in the root position; it occurs between the top two notes in the first inversion, between the middle two notes in the second inversion, and between the bottom two notes in the last inversion (see examples above). In extended position the student will have to rely solely on the sol-fa name of the bass note.

6 Recognition of a single four-part common chord as being in root position, first inversion or second inversion

If a student is preparing for an examination where he has to identify a single four-part chord as being in root position, first inversion or second inversion, without relation to a key, it is advisable to follow the method given in part 4 (*c*) above for chords in open position, thinking of the chord as being a tonic chord in each case (doh me soh, or doh maw soh).

But now a much lower bass note must be heard, as compared with the lowest note in the open position triads given in 4 (*c*). Students with a treble voice may find this hard. The teacher can help in the early stages by playing the bass note alone and asking such a student to sing it an octave higher; then playing the complete chord and asking the student to reproduce the bass note again.

The student will probably need practice in singing, aloud or mentally, the bass note of any chord (which can be taken at random from parts 6 and 7) before thinking of its identification.

Having learnt to hear the bass note he should now identify it as doh, producing a strong root position; me or maw, producing a weaker first inversion; or soh, producing a discord, requiring resolution.

Many arrangement of each of these chords are possible. Some are shown below:

But the student should realise that it is the *bass* note, in each case, that he needs to be able to recognise. Doh, me (maw) or soh can be at the top of any of these chords.

(*a*) Major common chords

In addition to the chords given below those given in part 7 (*a*) may also be used, but without the preliminary playing of the tonic chord.

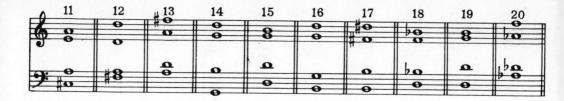

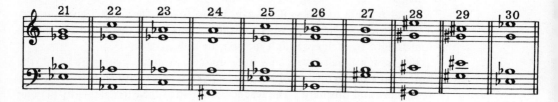

(b) Minor common chords

In addition to the chords given below those given in part 7 (b) may be used, but without the preliminary playing of the tonic chord.

The next stage is for major and minor common chords to be mixed together, using examples from (a) and (b) above.

7 Recognition of I, IV and V and their inversions, as single chords in four-part harmony, after the tonic chord has been played

This test means that nine chords have to be recognised, in relation to a tonic. Only one chord is given at a time, but the tonic chord in a suitable arrangement is played before it. Here is one arrangement of each of these chords in C major:

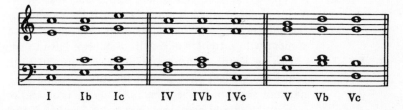

I	Ib	Ic	IV	IVb	IVc	V	Vb	Vc

Several other arrangements of each chord are possible, with different doubling and different notes at the top of the chord. But, as far as this test is concerned, all that the student needs to do is to identify the bass note and to recognise whether the chord is a root position or a first or second inversion.

If the above chords are written in order of an ascending bass line the following is discovered:

I or IVc	Vc	Ib	IV	V or Ic	IVb	Vb

From this it will be seen that only two bass notes, doh and soh, can carry two different chords; and, as one is a root position and the other a second inversion in each case, the aural difference is obvious, because the second inversion is a discord, requiring resolution.

If, then, the student can hear the bass note of each chord accurately he can name the chord by learning and applying the following table:

If the bass note is doh the chord is I or IVc

,, ,, ,, ,, ,, ray ,, ,, ,, Vc

,, ,, ,, ,, ,, me ,, ,, ,, Ib

,, ,, ,, ,, ,, fah , ,, ,, IV

,, ,, ,, ,, ,, soh ,, ,, ,, V or Ic

,, ,, ,, ,, ,, lah ,, ,, ,, IVb

,, ,, ,, ,, ,, te ,, ,, ,, Vb

The student will probably need practice in learning to hear the lowest note though, if he has worked at least a part of Sections V and VI and part 6 of this Section, his aural perception of a bass note should have made progress. He should lose no opportunity of trying to follow the bass part in any music he hears or plays.

The teacher may help by playing, for example, 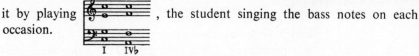 and following

it by playing ♪, the student singing the bass notes on each
occasion.

He can follow the same method with all the chords which follow.

Another helpful preliminary is for the teacher to play a slow-moving
series of chords (which may, if wished, be chosen from Section VIII) while
the student sings the bass note after each chord, without identifying it. A
student with a treble voice will, of course, have to sing it an octave higher.

Having learnt to hear and mentally reproduce the bass note after the
tonic, the student should then identify it, using sol-fa, and decide on the
name of the chord, when there is a choice (doh and soh).

Then he should check his answer by deciding if the chord did sound like
a root position or a first or second inversion, as the case may be.

In many cases the student may find it easier to hear these chords in a
progression, following the bass line as a melody, and to work through
Section VIII, parts 1–3.

Naturally he will find this test much easier if he has learnt to write and to
play the chords concerned. Writing, playing and hearing chord progressions
should be learnt at the same time.

(a) *Major keys*   The tonic chord is played in a suitable arrangement before each chord to
be identified. The following exercises do not always have this tonic chord
with the tonic at the top. But the teacher can re-arrange it if he wishes.

114

(b) *Minor keys*   The chords in C minor are:

I   Ib   Ic   IV   IVb   IVc   V   Vb   Vc

The possible chords on an ascending bass scale are:

I or IVc   Vc   Ib   IV   V or Ic   IVb   Vb

In a major key all the chords are major; but in a minor key I and IV are minor while V is major. This, therefore, makes recognition of chords in a minor key easier, because there is an additional helpful factor: if the chord is heard as major it *must* be V.

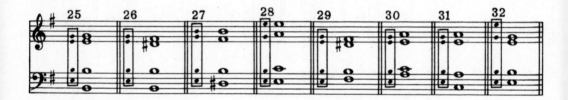

The next stage is to mix major and minor examples together, using (*a*) and
(*b*) above.

Section VIII
Chord Progressions

VARIOUS
EXAMINATION
REQUIREMENTS
Only one Practical Examination Board requires the recognition of chords in a progression. They ask for the recognition of I, IV and V in a succession of three chords, which is covered in part 1 below.

One C.S.E. Board requires the recognition of the recurrence of three harmonies. They are likely to be I, IV and V, though they might be I, II and V, or I, VI and V, as these combinations of chords are used fairly frequently for simple accompaniments to folk tunes or popular songs, perhaps played on the guitar. All that is required is that the pupil recognises that a chord he has heard earlier in the music recurs. This is not, therefore, identification by naming, nor is the music likely to be a passage in four-part harmony. Examples set in previous examinations should be studied in order to see the type of question, and should be used as tests for the examination candidates. Having discovered the type the teacher should easily find similar material.

Most G.C.E. Examinations require the naming of chords in a four-part progression at O Level, though the detailed requirements vary considerably. They are all, however, covered in parts 2–6 below. Unlike a practical examination, which requires an immediate oral answer, the candidate has to write the answer down, and thus has time to think, and to write down the melody and the bass as a help, if he wishes, as suggested below.

One or two of the G.C.E. Boards require the bass, or the melody and the bass to be written for O Level, in addition to naming the chords.

But even if the names only are required the candidate will often find it safer to write down the melody and the bass, because both help to check that the chord is correct. If the key is given these notes can be written on the staff. If not, the melody can be written in sol-fa, while roman numerals indicate the bass. The candidate who thinks he has heard te in the melody and IV in the bass knows that one of these surmises must be wrong, and can adjust accordingly.

At A Level all the Boards require the recognition of chords in a four-part progression, though again the detailed requirements vary. They are all, however, covered in parts 4–9 below. Most of the Boards require the outer parts to be written and the chords to be named or indicated by means of a figured bass. But a few Boards require the names of the chords only, even at A Level. There is no doubt, however, at this stage, that it is better for the candidate to write down the melody and the bass, as a check, to see that they fit, even though only the names are required.

One practical diploma examination asks for the recognition of I, IV and V and their inversions, which is covered in part 3 below.

Class music diploma examination requirements are similar to those for G.C.E. A Level.

Chord recognition tests at university level could be expected to include chromatic harmony, as in part 10 below.

Harmonic recognition should be an integral part of harmony teaching. As each new chord is learnt and applied in chord progressions, it should be written, played if possible, and also recognised by ear. But as no two harmony books agree as to the order in which chords should be learnt, it is impossible in this book to introduce each new chord separately, in suitable progressions, as each is learnt. The teacher should improvise his own tests, or use the examples given in the harmony book he is using.

The order given below is logical, though several new chords are added in each successive part. However, each part coincides with some examination requirement, and marks another stage in the development of aural harmonic perception.

1 I, IV and V in root position

There are three helpful means at the disposal of the student who wishes to recognise these chords.

The first, and most important, is to be able to hear the melodic line of the bass part, and to be able to sing it to sol-fa names. The teacher should play

and get the student to sing it to sol-fa names, an octave higher for a singer with a treble voice.

Then he should play

and get the student to sing the bass again, listening keenly for the lowest part, rather than just reproducing what he sang before.

Any of the following tests can be treated in the same way, if necessary.

As the student's hearing improves the complete passage can be played first, the student then singing the bass and finally checking by singing it again when the teacher plays it alone.

Secondly, the student should become aware of the different mental effect of the three chords. The tonic chord, I, is stronger than the other two, whatever note is at the top, and the student should soon be able to recognise it as the central, home chord of the key. The dominant chord, V, is bright and unfinished; and if the student sings te he will always find it is part of the chord. The subdominant chord, IV, is heavier and less bright than V, but not as strong and finished as I; and if the student is not sure whether the chord is IV or V and sings te he will realise it is *not* part of IV.

Thirdly, the student can sing the melody to sol-fa, as a check to see if it fits with the bass. He should learn the following table, if he has not already done so:

If the melody note is				doh	the chord		can be I or IV
,, ,,	,,	,,	,,	ray	,,	,,	is V
,, ,,	,,	,,	,,	me	,,	,,	,, I
,, ,,	,,	,,	,,	fah	,,	,,	,, IV
,, ,,	,,	,,	,,	soh	,,	,,	can be I or V
,, ,,	,,	,,	,,	lah	,,	,,	is IV
,, ,,	,,	,,	,,	te	,,	,,	,, V

Even at this stage it is a help to write the melody and bass to see that they fit. If the key has not been given the student can write the above progression as: D' D' T D'
I IV V I

This is a useful preparation for later tests, containing more chords.

If the answer has to be given orally, as in a practical examination, and the student has no paper to write on, he can still 'think' the above scheme for melody and bass.

The rhythm of the tests given in the whole of this Section is very simple; and the student should be encouraged to write down the correct note lengths and add the bar lines, in all the tests he writes down. But whether he uses the minim or the crotchet as the beat is a matter of indifference.

Minor keys

2 I, Ib, Ic, IV and V

Two G.C.E. Examination Boards set the above combination of chords for O Level. The chords are required to be named only, and the first chord is always in root position.

The following progression includes all these chords in C major:

The teacher should play this progression several times for the student to become familiar with its sound. He should learn the following:

Doh in the bass must be I
Me ,, ,, ,, ,, ,, Ib
Fah ,, ,, ,, ,, ,, IV
Soh ,, ,, ,, can be Ic or V

But if Ic is heard it will certainly be followed by V (forming a cadential $^6_4$ $^3_5$ progression). So a repeated bass note with a change of chord above it must be Ic V, which is therefore easily recognised (V Ic is unmusical, and would never be given).

It should perhaps be pointed out that a repeated bass note could occur

with two positions of the same chord:  But the student

should be able to tell that the second chord does not consist of different notes, but merely of the same notes rearranged.

In both of the examples given above the second G in the bass could also fall an octave, instead of being repeated at the same pitch.

As far as the mental effect of the chords is concerned there are two new chords to recognise, as compared with part 1 above. Ib, a first inversion, is weaker than any of the root positions; and Ic, a second inversion is a discord, requiring a resolution.

If the student learns to hear the bass line as a melody and is able to sing it to sol-fa, and then checks what he has written by reference to the mental effect of each chord, he should soon become sure of these chords. But a further check is provided by listening to the melody to see if it fits. As suggested in part 1 above, it is a help to write down both the melody and the bass, on the staff if the key is given; by using sol-fa for the melody and roman numerals for the bass if the key is not given.

3 Primary triads and their inversions

Every note of the scale can now be a bass note for one of the primary triads, in root position or inversion:

C major

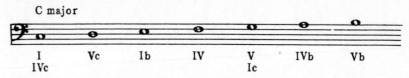

I	Vc	Ib	IV	V	IVb	Vb
IVc				Ic		

It will be noticed that doh and soh are the only two notes for which a choice is possible. Doh can carry IVc I, the cadential $^6_4$ $^5_3$ sometimes called the the organist's cadence:

IVc   I

Soh can also carry the cadential $^6_4$ $^5_3$, the more usual Ic V:

Ic   V

Both cadential $^6_4$ $^5_3$ progressions can be recognised by the change of chord over a repeated bass note.

The passing $^6_4$ can also occur in the following progressions:

I   Vc   Ib   IV   Ic   IVb

Notice that soh can be the bass note of both a cadential and a passing $^6_4$, though the effect is quite different.

If the student can hear and identify the bass note he should have little difficulty in recognising all these chords, particularly if he has learnt to use them in his harmony studies.

Having named the chord he should then check to see if the chord does sound like a strong root position, a weak first inversion, or a discordant second inversion; and a second check can be obtained, as suggested in parts 1 and 2, if he writes down the melody as well, to see if it fits with the bass.

4 Progressions containing major and minor common chords and their inversions

Some G.C.E. A Level examinations ask for the names of chords using these progressions.

It should be realised that this requirement precludes the inclusion of any diminished and augmented triads, even such frequently-used chords as VIIb in major and minor keys and IIb in the minor key.

The only second inversions that can reasonably be expected are those of primary triads, which have already been introduced in part 3.

Chords such as III and IIIb in the major key, and VIb in the major and minor key, though they are common chords are so rarely used that they are not very likely to occur in the easier examinations of this type; and some examinations definitely preclude them. A few examples are, however, given below, from 12 onwards.

Therefore the following are the possibilities in the major key, with the chords in brackets being rather unlikely:

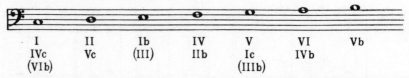

I	II	Ib	IV	V	VI	Vb
IVc	Vc	(III)	IIb	Ic	IVb	
(VIb)				(IIIb)		

If one assumes that only the harmonic form of the minor scale will be used, a reasonable assumption at this stage, then the possibilities in the minor key

126

are even narrower. It will be seen that the second, third, fourth and seventh degrees of the scale can only carry one chord. In fact, VI, and possibly VIb are the only chords additional to those given in part 3.

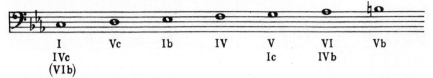

However, previous examination papers should be studied to see if chords using the melodic minor are included, as they could come into this category. A few are given below (18–21).

There are now many new chords as compared with part 3. As each new chord is introduced in the harmony lesson, ear tests on it, in comparison with other, similar chords should be given. For example, the following should be compared:

127

5 Progressions containing any diatonic triads and their inversions

This stage adds diminished and augmented triads to the vocabulary.

IIb in the minor key, the first inversion of a diminished triad, is used just as freely in the minor key as in the major, when it is a minor triad, and in the same kind of progressions:

VIIb, in both major and minor keys, is frequently used, particularly in the following progressions:

Notice that (b) and (c) above can only be used in the minor key if the melodic minor is used, A♭ becoming A♮

IIIb in the minor key is also fairly common:

129

The root positions of the diminished and augmented triads are less frequently used, and it is common to prepare and resolve the fifth:

II   III   VII

If an examination asks for all diatonic triads and inversions it is nevertheless unlikely that the above progressions will frequently be used, except for IIb in the minor key, and VIIb in the major and minor key.

6 Progressions containing any diatonic triads and their inversions, and the root position of the dominant seventh

Those G.C.E. O Level examinations which include written harmony as an integral part of their examination very reasonably require the same vocabulary of chords for written harmony and for aural recognition. A passage containing five or six chords is usually given. One Board asks for the names only, another Board asks for the names and the bass notes, while a third Board requires the melody and the bass, as well as the names. The actual vocabulary varies slightly, and one Board only requires progressions in the major key. But, on the whole, their requirements correspond to this part, part 6.

As compared with part 5, the only new chord for recognition is the root position of the dominant seventh. It has the same bass note as V, and occurs in similar places, except that it would not end a phrase. It has four different notes, as compared with three, fah being the extra note. But the chief difference, and the one that the student should make use of, for purposes of comparison, is that V is a concord whereas ⁷V is a discord.

A number of tests of five or six chords are given below, using the more usual progressions, and avoiding the unusual progressions given in part 5, because this is the kind of test that is most likely to be given for O Level—⁷V is much more frequently used than III or VII. Therefore many of these tests are easier than those given in part 5.

If the student has to write the melody and the bass, as well as naming the chords, it is suggested that he works as follows:

(1) Write the melody on the staff, thinking in sol-fa, and taking care to start on the right note of the scale.

(2) Write the bass in the same way.

(3) Look at the two, to see how they fit, what intervals they make, and what chords they are likely to imply. While waiting for the next hearing, it might be wise to pencil in the possibilities.

(4) At the next hearing, listen carefully to each chord, judging by impression in relation to the key, and deciding whether each chord is a root position or a first or second inversion, a concord or a discord. Write the roman numerals under each bass note. (Some teachers and some examinations may prefer to express this by means of a figured bass. But 6 merely shows a first inversion, whereas Ib or VIIb is much more explicit, and incidentally shows the examiner that the candidate is aware of the big difference between the sound of these two first inversions.)

The teacher should play the chords slowly and deliberately, so that the student has time to take in the progression of each chord.

7 Progressions containing any diatonic triads and their inversions, and the dominant seventh and its inversions

This stage corresponds to some A Level examinations and one class music diploma. One A Level examination asks for the melody and bass of a single chant.

As compared with part 6 this part includes the inversions of the dominant seventh.

These usually resolve on to I or Ib, and they often occur between two positions of the tonic chord. ⁷Vb with te in the bass will rise to doh; ⁷Vc with ray in the bass can move to doh or me (the latter containing the rising seventh); ⁷Vd with fah in the bass will fall to me. Also one position of a dominant seventh can move to another, the last one resolving.

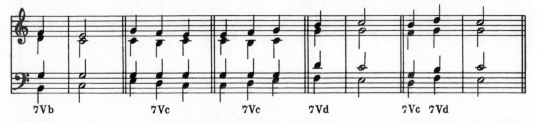

A 'passing' effect can also occur between two positions of the dominant seventh with IVb or IVc in between (see (a) and (b) below). And ⁷V, ⁷Vb or ⁷Vc can resolve on to IVc I, instead of I, just as could V or Vb, in the 'organist's' cadence (see (c) and (d) below).

The inversions of the dominant seventh produce a considerable enlargement of the vocabulary; and many other arrangements, with different notes in the treble are available, in addition to those shown above. The student should learn to hear them at the same time as he learns to write and play them.

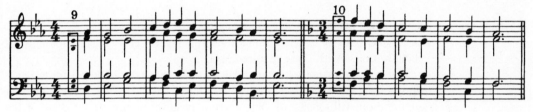

Single Chants

8 Simple progressions including modulation to related keys

Several G.C.E. A Level examinations and several class music diplomas set dictation tests with these requirements.

The new factor is that of modulation. The passage is nearly sure to begin and end in the same key; and if it is fairly short the most likely kind of modulation will consist of ^{7}V I, in root position or inverted, in one of the related keys. The following all begin in C major.

The student should hear and recognise the movement in both the melody and the bass, and then analyse the resultant dominant seventh, deciding which position it is in. He should first have learnt how to modulate in this way himself, and should thus get familiar with the sound of the most common modulations. The teacher may find it helpful to play the above examples several times, for purposes of comparison, telling the student what they are.

Examples 13–16 modulate to more than one key.

Examples 17–27 establish a new key, in a more leisurely way, by means of a pivot chord. The shorter ones remain in that key; the longer ones (23–27) return to the tonic key. A study of Section X should prove helpful if this kind of test is required.

9 Progressions including any diatonic chords, including suspensions, and modulation

Those teachers who wish ear tests to keep pace with their pupil's growing harmonic vocabulary will be glad of the following tests. They correspond to some G.C.E. requirements at A Level, and should also be useful for music students in colleges and universities.

This part includes diatonic sevenths, the higher dominant discords, and suspensions.

10 Progressions including chromatic harmony

A few tests including chromatic harmony are added, for those students in colleges or universities who may need them.

Section IX
Cadences

A few C.S.E. Boards ask for the recognition of cadences, though one Board gives them in major keys only.

All the Practical Examination Boards require the recognition of cadences in their higher grades. Some confine their first tests to major keys, while others harmonise the cadences only, the melody leading to the cadence being unharmonised. One Board confines its first tests to recognition of perfect and plagal cadences, while another Board plays the tonic chord and then the cadence, which is, in effect, a chord ear test of the kind given in Section VIII.

Some Boards grade their tests so that, at first, only one cadence is given at a time, while a sentence containing two, three or four cadences is given at later stages. One Board states that I V is the only kind of imperfect cadence to be recognised, others confine their cadences to chords in root position, while yet others discriminate between their grades by having their cadences without decoration in earlier grades and with decoration at a more advanced stage.

At O Level one G.C.E. Board gives the cadences preceded by a tonic chord only, that is, a chord, rather than a cadence test. Another Board states that no inverted cadences will be required. One Board confines its tests to two phrases, while others give a sentence which may contain three or four cadences.

But half the O Level examinations do not give cadence tests as such, preferring to give chord recognition tests as in Section VIII.

At A Level only two Boards give cadence tests. The rest require the recognition of chords in a continuous passage instead (see Section VIII).

Those diploma examinations which give cadence tests may require three, four or five cadences in a continuous passage, and the cadences may be decorated or inverted.

In view of the great variety described above in grading cadence recognition tests it seems advisable to divide the tests in this Section according to the chords involved, and to give tests in parts 1–3 in the following ways: (1) a tonic chord followed by the cadence; (2) a single melodic phrase ending with harmonised cadence; (3) a single harmonised phrase ending with a cadence; (4) a continuous harmonised passage containing two, three or four cadences. The part 4 cadence tests, being more elaborate, are only given in a harmonised passage containing two or more cadences.

Teachers can, however, adapt all the tests which follow to their own requirements, by adding or deleting melodies or harmonies, changing minor key examples to major and vice versa. In this way they can plan their own course of testing, using the examples given below in many ways. In the early stages it is often helpful to play the bass of the cadence chords in octaves.

1 Perfect and imperfect cadences in root position

These two cadences are the ones most frequently found, and they are more easily differentiated from each other than are the others. So it is sensible to learn to recognise them first.

A phrase ending with I has the tonic in the bass. It may or may not sound very finished, as this depends also upon the arrangement of the melody notes. But the student should learn to listen to the bass, and to recognise the presence of the tonic as the last bass note.

A phrase ending with V has the dominant in the bass, and usually sounds less finished than a perfect cadence, though again it is coloured by the shape of the melody. The student should feel, however, that V could not end a a piece of music: another phrase is required to finish it off.

If he has carried the sound of the tonic in his mind while the passage has been played he should be able to tell that doh is not the last bass note. Also, if he sings te to himself, he will find it fits with the final chord, when this is V.

But, as with all tests involving harmony, the ability to hear and recognise the bass note is the most important factor. Methods of recognising the lowest note of an interval or chord have already been suggested in Sections V, VI, VII and VIII, so should not need repetition here.

(a) Tonic chord followed by I V or V I

The student should listen carefully to the preliminary tonic chord, and decide whether the first chord of the cadence he hears consists of the same notes (though perhaps in a different arrangement) or whether it is a completely different chord, with a different bass note.

(b) *A single melodic phrase followed by I V or V I*

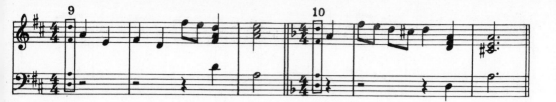

(c) A single harmonised phrase followed by an imperfect cadence (any chord before V) or a perfect cadence

At this stage, when only perfect and imperfect cadences have to be recognised and differentiated, it is only the last bass note of the phrase that needs to be recognised. So II V is no more difficult than I V; and ^{7}V I no more difficult than V I.

147

(d) A continuous passage containing 2, 3 or 4 perfect or imperfect cadences

2 Perfect and plagal cadences in root position

This is rather more difficult than part I, as both cadences end with the tonic chord. Now the student must listen keenly to the pentultimate chord.

Both cadences can sound more or less final, according to the movement of the melody. There are four helpful ways of telling the difference between them:

1. V I is much more common than IV I, and usually therefore sounds more natural.

2. V I usually has a brighter effect than IV I (IV I is normally used for 'Amen').

3. If you sing te doh at the same time as the cadence it will fit with V I, but not with IV I.

4. V I has soh doh in the bass, while IV I has fah doh.

The last method (4) is the most helpful and reliable way of telling the difference. So, again, listening down to the bass notes is the most important factor.

In the minor key it is also helpful to realise that the penultimate chord, IV, in the plagal cadence is minor, while in the perfect cadence the penultimate chord, V, is major.

It is perhaps rather easier to feel the general impression of the cadence if it is heard after a completed phrase, rather than just a tonic chord. But both types of test are included here, as either may be required for examination purposes.

(a) Tonic chord followed by a perfect or plagal cadence

(b) A single melodic phrase followed by a perfect or plagal cadence

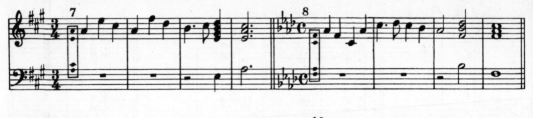

(c) A single harmonised phrase followed by a perfect or plagal cadence

(d) A continuous passage containing 2, 3 or 4 perfect or plagal cadences

153

3 All four cadences in root position

The additional cadence to the three that have been studied in parts 1 and 2 is the interrupted cadence. In this the ear recognises V as the penultimate chord and is led to expect I, making a perfect cadence. But some other chord takes its place, thus creating a greater or less sense of surprise or interruption, according to the chord used. It is frequently VI, but it may be a chromatic discord, creating a greater sense of surprise, and perhaps even leading to a change of key.

Most students find the interrupted cadence the easiest to recognise; and, after a few preliminary demonstrations, it should not require separate practice, but can be taken in conjunction and comparison with the other three cadences.

When working tests in cadence recognition students are recommended to think in the following way:

1. Decide whether or not the last chord has the tonic in the bass.

2. If it has, the cadence must be perfect or plagal. The student then listens to the penultimate chord, and follows the method outlined in part 2.

3. If it has not, the student next decides whether the cadence contains an element of surprise, and listens for V as the penultimate chord. In this way he recognises the interrupted cadence.

4. Any other cadence is imperfect. (Occasionally imperfect cadences are found which do not end on V, but they are unlikely to be given in elementary ear tests. I IV is fairly common.) The recognition of V, either as the final or the penultimate chord is the deciding factor in distinguishing between interrupted and imperfect cadences. Both cadences sound unfinished, but their effect is quite different.

(a) *Tonic chord followed by a cadence*

Eight are given in each key, each meant to be preceded by the tonic chord.

(b) A single melodic phrase ending with a harmonised cadence
　　　Five varied endings to each beginning are given.

(c) A single harmonised phrase ending with a cadence

Four varied endings to each phrase are given.

(d) A continuous passage containing 2, 3 or 4 cadences

Adagio

4 All four cadences in more elaborate forms

In more advanced examinations cadences are presented for recognition in more elaborate forms. The melody or harmony may be decorated, perhaps by cadential $^6_4$s or suspensions; and the penultimate chord is frequently inverted, though the final chord is still usually in its root position, in this kind of test. But, of course, either or both chords may be inverted in an inverted cadence.

163

The following are all forms of perfect cadences:

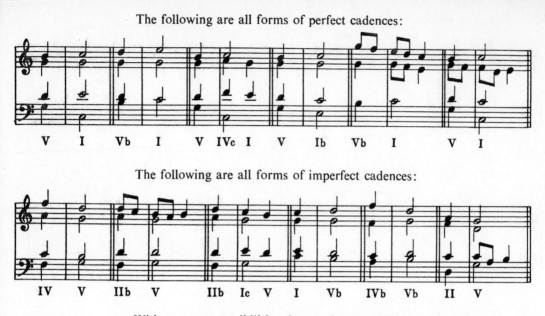

| V | I | Vb | I | V | IVc | I | V | Ib | Vb | I | V | I |

The following are all forms of imperfect cadences:

| IV | V | IIb | V | IIb | Ic | V | I | Vb | IVb | Vb | II | V |

With so many possibilities these cadences really become a form of chord ear test, and are thus better studied in Section VIII. It is for this reason that many A Level examinations give a succession of chords rather than a cadence ear test.

But if, as is usual, the final chord is still in its root position, the four steps outlined in part 3 can still be followed. When deciding between perfect and plagal it is still helpful to sing te doh at the same time as the cadence, to see if it fits. And the distinction between imperfect and interrupted still applies.

Naturally, however, the student who can recognise, in full, the two final chords, is at an advantage.

So far, in this book, it has seemed better to write ear tests exactly suited to the stage the student has reached, rather than to search for examples from the classics, which rarely fit so exactly; if they are suitable in one way, they are often too difficult in another.

It might be thought that the classics would provide suitable material for cadence ear tests. But, either they are so short and simple that the only cadences are perfect and imperfect; or—as is much more usual—they modulate by the third phrase.

However, it is possible to find a few hymns which can be used, though, again, most hymns modulate, and are therefore too difficult at this stage. Five are given here (Nos. 18–22). The following tunes are also suitable and can be found in most hymn books:

(a) *Containing two varieties of cadence:* Arfon; Ellacombe; St. Albinus; Stuttgart; Wiltshire.

165

166

St. David

Duke Street

172

St. Peter

Simeon

Helmsley

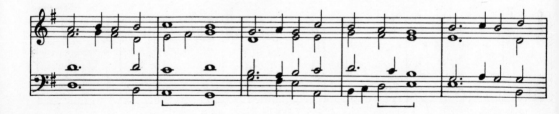

Section X
Key and Modulation

VARIOUS
EXAMINATION
REQUIREMENTS

Several C.S.E. Boards ask the candidate to state whether an extract played to them is in the major or minor mode (see part 1). A few Boards also ask candidates to name the modulations in a passage which is played to them and of which they have the copy. But this is visual, as well as aural, recognition, and is covered in Section XII. There is no recognition of modulation solely by ear.

One grade VIII practical examination requires the recognition of a modulation to the dominant or subdominant major or the relative minor from a major key (see part 2). Some diploma examinations ask for this, and also for a similar recognition from a minor key with its corresponding relationships (see parts 2 and 3). One diploma examination asks for the recognition of modulation to nearly-related keys in a hymn tune of six to eight phrases (see part 6).

Five of the eight G.C.E. Boards do not, at present, require the aural recognition of modulation at O Level. One Board asks for the recognition of a modulation to the dominant or subdominant major or the relative minor from a major key (see part 2). Another asks for a similar recognition in a passage starting in a major or minor key, three extracts being given, each containing one modulation, and each starting in the same way (see parts 2 and 3). One Board asks for the recognition of modulation to 'an attendant key'. This probably means the five most nearly-related keys and is covered in parts 4 and 5.

At A Level there are three Boards which do not ask for the recognition of modulation as a separate ear test, though one of these Boards may give a passage which modulates as a chord dictation ear test. The other Boards require recognition of modulation to the five most closely-related keys. But some Boards give one modulation at a time (see parts 4 and 5), while others give a series of modulations (usually not more than three) in a continuous passage. This is considerably more difficult and is covered in part 6.

1 Recognising whether a passage is in the major or the minor mode

The essential difference between the major and the minor mode is the difference in the third degree of the scale. C major contains a major third and a corresponding major tonic triad: ;

and C minor contains a minor third and a corresponding minor tonic triad:

The differences in the top tetrachord, which has several forms, one being just like the tonic major, do not affect the issue, and can be ignored by the student who is just learning to recognise major versus minor mode. His notational knowledge of the variants of harmonic and melodic minor, if he has it, may even cause him unnecessary confusion.

The presence of this major or minor third is most commonly recognised in the tonic chord, which is usually the first or second chord of the passage and almost certainly the last. (The major third in the last chord of a piece in a minor key, the tierce de Picardie, very commonly used by Bach and his contemporaries, would not be given in an elementary test of this nature.)

There is also a difference in general impression which most students easily feel. Play the National anthem in major and minor mode as an illustration of this:

But it is dangerous to express this feeling by such terms as happy or sad, because this depends so much on other factors: speed, rhythmic figures, tonal intensity and so on. For this reason it is important to play the above examples at exactly the same speed and intensity, so that the essential melodic and harmonic changes are the only ones that are heard.

The following song is in the minor key, but sounds bright and vigorous:

Charlie is my Darling

Having played this, play it in the major, when it will be heard to be even more bright and vigorous:

Then play the two examples again, in both forms, drawing attention to the major and minor triads as the first and last chords of each extract, and asking the student to sing the chord to sol-fa names, after the passage has been played, in each case.

Further examples can be played by the teacher, turning a major extract into a minor and vice versa, if the student needs more practice.

There is no need to write special examples for this kind of test. The teacher can play any music he likes, provided that it stays in one key and that minor pieces do not end with a tierce de Picardie. Some of the examples given in Section IX may be suitable, if the teacher does not want to look further afield, particularly those in the (*d*) sections of parts 1 and 2. (The teacher should change the final chord to minor of any minor key examples that end with a tierce de Picardie.) Examples given in part 3 (*d*) or part 4 may also be used, provided that they end with the tonic chord and that the tierce de Picardie is avoided or changed.

2 Recognising single modulations from a major key to the dominant or subominant major or the relative minor

Before giving the student any modulation ear tests he should clearly understand what modulation is, and also what is meant by 'related key'. An example such as the following can be played. Ending (*a*) sounds so natural and so closely-related that some students may hardly realise it has modulated at all. It might be compared to visiting the house of a close relative. Ending (*b*), though pleasant, sounds more remote: most students will now be aware of modulation and will also realise that the key is less closely-related than (*a*). It might be compared with a visit from England to Scotland. Ending (*c*) sounds very abrupt and not related at all. It might be compared with a visit from England to China. Of course, modulation to any key is possible. and does not need to be as clumsy as (*c*). Sometimes an unexpected modulation can sound very lovely. But modulation to distantly-related keys always sounds more remote, even if well-managed, and it is more difficult to return to the tonic key centre. It was rarely used by the earlier classical composers.

The teacher should then go on to explain to the student that, technically, relationship between keys depends upon the number of notes that they have in common. C major is related to G major because one only note of the scale is different and has to be changed. (Example (*a*) above.) E minor has two or three different notes. (Example (*b*) above.) But C ♯ major has no note in common with C major, unless E ♯ and B ♯ are enharmonically changed to F and C. (Example (*c*) above.)

The three most closely-related keys to a major key centre are the three that require only one note to be changed to reach the new key. They are: (*a*) modulation to the dominant major, requiring fah to be changed to fe; (*b*) modulation to the sub-dominant major, requiring te to be changed to taw; and (*c*) modulation to the relative minor, requiring soh to be changed to se. The teacher should demonstrate this by comparing the scales of C major with G major, F major and A minor. The student should learn to think of these relationships, using relative-pitch names. 'Modulation to the dominant (the soh key) by means of fe' applies to every key, whereas 'modulation from C major to G major by means of F♯' applies to only one key.

The teacher should then play the three examples given below, as a preliminary demonstration of the effect of these three modulations from C major.

There are two main ways of recognising these three modulations. One is by general impression, and the other is by listening for particular notes and relating them to the two keys concerned. After the student has become familiar with the various effects by hearing sufficient examples (and preferably also by learning to write them himself) he will usually recognise these modulations at once by the general impression. But if he is wise he will then check his impression by more detailed listening, more particularly to the bass.

General impression. Modulation from a major key to its dominant major can be recognised in three ways:

1. It usually sounds brighter than the other two with which it is, at present, being compared. Play the example with the three endings given above as an illustration of this.

2. It sounds very natural: most simple pieces in the major key modulate to the dominant and back. A brief excursion to the dominant may even sound very like an imperfect cadence in the tonic key.

3. There is a strong desire to return immediately to the tonic key. The final chord, I, of the dominant key is the same as V of the tonic key; and if the teacher plays V I of C major at the completion of (*a*) given above, or plays the opening bars again, the student will realise how naturally they follow on. Thereafter the student should mentally sing V I of the tonic key, or the opening bars of the passage for himself, as a method of recognising this modulation.

Modulation from a major key to its subdominant major can similarly be recognised in three ways:

1. It is usually less bright and often rather solemn and heavy as compared to modulation to the dominant. Again, play examples 1. and 2. above, in comparison.

2. It is not at all common as the *only* modulation in a piece of music. It occurs in the latter sections of a piece which modulates to several keys: a matter which is not, at present, under consideration. So the student will feel that it sounds unusual and rather remote.

3. There is no great desire to return to the tonic key immediately. One may even have forgotten the sound of V I in the tonic key. Illustrate this by playing V I in C major, or the opening bars after playing the modulation given above. Thereafter the student should make this test for himself.

Modulation from a major key to its relative minor is rarely mistaken for the two to the major keys mentioned above, as it ends in a minor key, and most students at this stage can recognise this. Again compare the three given above, paying particular attention, this time, to the final chord.

Detailed listening. The following two methods may be used:

1. The student with a good ear may try to detect the presence of fe, taw or se, as a check to the general impression received. However it *may* not be present and, certainly, it is not always present in the tune. The student may be able to detect these three chromatic notes in the tune in the examples given above. But this is quite difficult, and the teacher may prefer to say little or nothing about this. (It assumes that the student can easily follow and recognise each note of the complete melodic line.)

2. More important is to remember the tonic of the original key, to sing the tonic of the new key (which means hearing the bass note) and then singing from the one to the other by step. This, for many students, is quite difficult, but it is the one sure way of checking the result; so the student should persevere, with the help of the teacher. Care should be taken to call the *first* tonic doh, and to sing up or down from this to the second tonic. The other way round will, of course, produce the wrong result.

All the examples given below have three or four endings, each modulating to one of the three related keys. At first the teacher may like to give them one after the other, for the purposes of comparison. But, at a later stage, he should play only one of each at a time and then move to a different example.

Some examinations give the same beginning, modulating to different keys, while others give a different beginning in each case. Also, it must be realised that, in an examination, the same modulation may be given twice. This is why there are some examples given below which go to the same key twice.

When the examiner states the key from which the passage is to start the student should immediately name the three keys to which he may modulate; and, if the test is a written one, he will be wise to make a note of them at the bottom of his paper. It is surprising how often a student gives the name of a key to which the music could not possibly modulate!

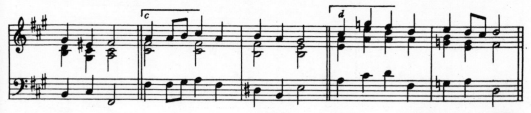

3 Recognising single modulations from a minor key to the dominant or subdominant minor or the relative major

The three most closely-related keys to a minor key centre are usually considered to be the dominant and subdominant minor and the relative major.

But the effects are surprisingly different from the three modulations discussed in part 2, the three from a major key centre. Now, the modulation to the relative major is the brightest, most natural and most common. It is also the easiest to recognise because it is the only one of the three which ends in a major key, and therefore with an easily-recognised major triad. Very few students mistake it for either of the other two modulations.

Modulation to the dominant and subdominant minor, as the only modulation in a short piece, are both comparatively rare. They each require two notes to be changed, and they sound equally remote. It was discovered in part 2, when modulating from C major to G major, that the final chord, I, in G major was the same as V in C major; and it was simple and natural to return to C major by using the same chord, thinking of it as V in C major and following it by I in this key. But, when modulating from C minor to G minor, the final chord in G minor is a minor triad, G B♭ D, and is not usable as a lead-back to C minor unless the modulation ends with a tierce de Picardie, changing the final chord to G B♮ D.

However, some students, having decided that a modulation is to a minor key, may like to make a mental change of the final chord from minor to major to see if it sounds like V of the tonic key and can therefore be followed by I and a return to the opening. This will 'work' with modulation to the dominant, and not with modulation to the subdominant.

But the safest way to recognise the difference between these two modulations is to remember the first tonic and sing from it, by step, to the second tonic, as recommended in part 2.

The teacher should play the first example given below, telling the student the names of the three keys from C minor to which the music modulates, and discussing the effects and the methods of recognition.

4. Recognising single modulations from a major key to the five most closely-related keys

It is generally considered that the five most closely-related keys from any major or minor key centre are those which have not more than one sharp or flat more or less in the key signature. When starting from a major key these keys are the dominant and subdominant major and the relative minor of all three keys. Here are the related keys from C major:

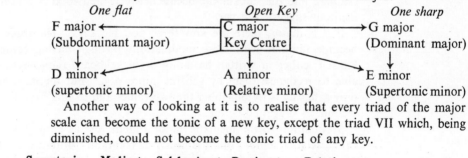

Another way of looking at it is to realise that every triad of the major scale can become the tonic of a new key, except the triad VII which, being diminished, could not become the tonic triad of any key.

It is easy to think of these as fah and soh major, ray me and lah minor. This can be applied to any major key centre. The student should make a list of the related keys to other major keys, for practice. He should always do this as a preliminary when the starting key of an extract is given, before he listens to the actual modulations.

Here are examples of modulation to the supertonic minor and the mediant minor, the two relationships which are new. They would be unlikely to occur as the only modulations in a piece of music, but would be part of a scheme including several modulations. They start the same way as the examples given for modulation to the dominant and subdominant major and relative minor in part 2. The teacher should now play all the five, for the student to compare their effects.

When being asked to recognise these five modulations the student should first decide whether the new key is major or minor. If it is major, it is already familiar, and the student can decide between the two keys concerned by the methods suggested in part 2.

If it is minor, there are now three possible keys. The student who has become familiar with these modulations through having composed them himself, either in written harmony or in keyboard improvisation, may be able to recognise them by general impression. But for most students the only safe way is to remember the two tonics and to sing from the first to the second, as suggested before.

Modulation to the mediant minor sounds just as natural as modulation to the relative minor, and it is nearly as common. Both involve the interval of a third between the two tonics, and students often confuse the two, usually because they carelessly call the second tonic doh instead of the first. For example, in modulation from C major to A minor the student should sing from C down to A—doh te lah. In modulation from C to E minor he should sing from C up to E—doh ray me. If he starts from E, by mistake, and sings down to C, falling a third, he may think the modulation is to the relative minor.

Modulation to the supertonic minor involves the interval of a second between the two tonics, and is therefore less likely to be confused with the other two.

The first five sets of examples given below are confined to modulations to the three minor keys, as comparisons between these three introduce the new factor which the student requires to recognise.

The later examples may modulate to any of the five related keys. But there is still a preponderance of modulation to the mediant and the super-tonic minor, the two new effects. The teacher can mix them with the modulations given in part 2, so as to preserve a balance.

5 Recognising single modulations from a minor key to the five most closely-related keys

The five most closely-related keys to a minor key centre are the dominant and sub-dominant minor and the relative major of all three keys. Here are the related keys from C Minor:

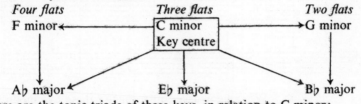

Here are the tonic triads of these keys, in relation to C minor:

It will be realised that these triads are not all built from the harmonic minor scale of the tonic key, in the way that the related keys to a major key centre were based on the major scale of the tonic key. Three of the triads, marked * above, use a B♭ which, though part of the melodic minor scale, is much less commonly used in chord formations in C minor than is B♮, the leading note, which plays such an important part in establishing a key.

Students who think in terms of doh minor in sol-fa can remember these five modulations by thinking of them as fah and soh minor and the three 'aws'—maw, law and taw major.

Students who think in terms of lah minor may prefer to look at the table shown at the beginning of part 4, transferring the term 'key centre' to A minor instead of C major. The five related keys to A minor are then the same as those shown on that plan.

But, whatever method he uses, the student should be given some preliminary practice in naming the five related keys to a number of minor key centres; and he should always do this before starting a modulation recognition test.

Here are examples of modulation to A♭ major and B♭ major from C minor, the two relationships which are new. They would be unlikely to occur as the only modulation in a piece of music, but would be part of a scheme including several modulations. They start the same way as the first example given in part 3. The teacher should now play all five, for the student to compare their effects.

When he is asked to recognise these five modulations the student should first decide whether the new key is major or minor. If it is minor it is already familiar, and the student can decide between the two keys concerned by the two methods suggested in part 3.

If it is major there are now three possible keys. Again, the only safe way is to remember the two tonics and to sing from the first to the second by step.

The first five sets of examples given below are confined to modulations to the three major keys. The rest modulate to any of the five keys, though there is still a preponderance of the two modulations which are new to the student, as compared with part 3. The teacher can mix them with the modulations in part 3, so as to preserve the balance.

6 Recognising two or three modulations to related keys in a continuous passage

Some teachers may prefer to work part (*b*) before (*a*). The examples are easier, because the return to the tonic key in the middle helps to keep the key centre in the student's mind. They are also a good preparation for working part (*a*). But modulation ear tests without a return to the tonic key in the middle are more commonly given in examinations, and are therefore dealt with first in this section. The sequential examples given as preliminaries in part (*a*) should also be helpful before working part (*c*).

(a) Three modulations to related keys without a return to the tonic key in the middle

This is much more difficult than hearing one modulation at a time. The student has to keep the key centre in his mind throughout a series of changes of key, and also hear the relationships between one related key and another.

The usual number of modulations in such an examination ear test is three. It is helpful to realise what is likely to happen.

In a four-phrased example the first phrase will probably establish the tonic key. The second phrase will contain the main modulation, probably

201

ending with a perfect cadence in root position. If the key centre is major this key is most frequently the dominant major, though it may be the relative minor. If the key centre is minor it will almost certainly modulate to the relative major, though the dominant minor is possible. The student is already familiar with all these effects.

The third phrase may contain two modulations, very often sequential; and the fourth phrase will re-establish the tonic key. Alternatively, the third phrase may only contain one modulation and the fourth phrase may quickly touch on the third modulation before returning to the tonic key.

It will be realised that it is the second half of the piece that contains the new aural experiences. And, although sequences are not inevitable, they are so very common that it will certainly be helpful for the student to familiarise himself with the most common effects.

Play the following example to the student. He will easily recognise the modulation to the dominant in bar 4. Then continue with the next bar, the modulation to E minor, and pause. Get him to sing the three tonics, C, G and E, and realise their relationship. Then go on to the next bar and get him to sing D. He should realise that: *1*. E and D are both minor keys; *2*. the sequence and therefore the modulation is a second lower; *3*. E and D are the only minor keys related to C major which are a second apart. Then continue to the end of the passage so that the student can relate D minor to the C major with which it ends.

Then play the following passage, which is identical except that the modulation in bar 4 is to the relative minor. Go through the same processes with this example.

202

Then play the following passage, which begins and ends in A minor and modulates to C major in bar 4, but contains the same keys, E minor and D minor, as transitional sequences in bars 5 and 6. Follow the same process outlined above. Now it is helpful to realise that E and D are the only minor keys, related to A minor, a second apart.

The following are a series of common sequential modulations which could all occur in bars 5 and 6 of a similar piece beginning and ending in C major or A minor. (The first one has been illustrated above.) They are deliberately made as simple as possible, for the purposes of illustration. Some will work with the same beginnings and endings as the three previous examples, while others may require modifications so as to produce a good join. (In some cases they may produce two modulations instead of three, because one of the keys is already present in the first half of the passage.) The teacher should make any necessary modifications or improvise his own beginnings and endings. Alternatively he can merely play V I in C major or A minor at the beginning and end of each example.

In each case a pause should be made after each modulation for the student to sing the appropriate tonics and relate them to each other, as outlined above. His reasoning should help his ear; having heard a sequence rising a fourth or falling a third he should realise what available keys have this relationship.

Obviously the student who has written such progressions himself, or can improvise them, is at an advantage. Familiarity, through hearing, writing or playing, will all help to establish these progressions in the student's mind.

(a) Falling or rising a second. Both minor

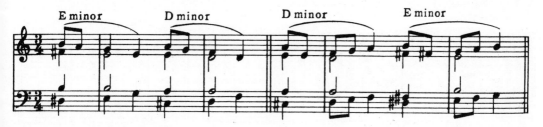

(b) Falling or rising a second. Both major

G major   F major   F major   G major

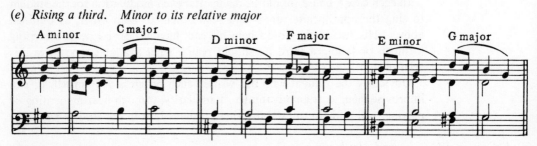

(c) Rising a second. Major to minor

G major   A minor

(d) Falling a second. Minor to major

A minor   G major

(e) Rising a third. Minor to its relative major

A minor   C major   D minor   F major   E minor   G major

(f) Falling a third. Major to its relative minor

C major   A minor   F major   D minor   G major   E minor

204

(g) Falling a third. Minor to major

(h) Rising a third. Major to minor

(i) Rising a fourth. Both major

(j) Rising a fourth. Both minor

The examples which follow all contain modulations to three different keys and include many examples of sequence. None of them return to the tonic key in the middle.

A teacher who has to prepare pupils for an examination that gives this kind of test should make use of as many 'back' papers as possible, so that the student gains familiarity with the requirements of his particular examination.

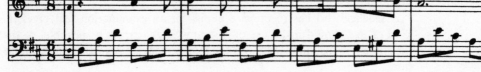

Menuetto

Haydn *String quartet* Op. 17 No. 6

Allegretto scherzando   Haydn *String quartet* Op. 33 No. 2

(b) Two modulations to related keys plus a return to the tonic key in the middle

It is very common to find music which returns to the tonic key at least once in the course of a passage. This is particularly prone to happen when the music has a major key as its centre. If it is in the dominant key at the end of the first half, as is customary, it is very natural to return to the tonic key before proceeding to further modulation.

Such a passage may contain modulations to two different keys but with a return to the tonic key in the middle, which therefore means that there are still three changes of key. This is less commonly given as an examination test, but the student should find it easier; the tonic key in the middle helps to keep the key centre in his mind.

Merton

Richmond

212

Prysgol

(c) *Three modulations to related keys plus a return to the tonic key in the middle*

It is quite common to find pieces which contain modulations to three different keys but also contain a return to the tonic key in the middle, thus producing four changes of key. Again, this is more common if the key centre is major.

213

Sometimes there is only one modulation in the first half and two modulations in the second; and sometimes it is the other way round. Both types are included here. In either case the main modulation, half way through, is usually established leisurely by means of a pivot chord, while the other modulations are merely transitions, usually consisting of V I in each related key.

Andante

Passion Chorale

St. Matthew

Section XI
Tests of General Musical Experience

This is a type of test which is being encouraged by the Department of Education and Science, in connection with the C.S.E. examination.

The tests are given by means of a tape or a gramophone record. The most usual kind consists of a series of short and very varied extracts, before and after which the candidate is asked a specific question about the music.

These types of question come under parts 1–8 given below. Questions on quite different subjects come quickly one after another; and, at present, little material is available, apart from the Department's specimen tests and the few tests previously set by the various C.S.E. Boards.

Accordingly this Section consists mostly of suggestions to the teacher as to how he can best use his existing school records for this purpose. The suggestions are based on records, some of which, at least, the teacher will have in his school library; and he can make up similar questions on other records he happens to possess.

It is sound practice to encourage pupils to listen for a specific point or series of points when listening to most records. It encourages keen listening and prevents the pupil's mind from wandering or day-dreaming. So it is a good plan to give a class a series of questions before a record starts, and ask for the answers after it has finished. This should not *always* be done, of course; there are occasions, particularly at the end of a lesson, when listening to a record for pure enjoyment should take place. But, in general, there is much to be said for focusing the pupils' attention on certain particular aspects of the music. The teacher should think out suitable questions beforehand, and make a list of them for future reference.

The teacher who possesses a tape-recorder and is willing to spend time on his work would be well advised to prepare special tapes containing a number of short extracts from his existing records, with spoken questions before and after each record, similar to those issued by the Department of Education and Science and to those given in parts 1–8 below. The tapes, once prepared, can be used again and again for successive groups of students, so that the teacher's work will save time in the future. (The playing of a gramophone record or tape is restricted to its private or educational use, but teachers should consult any existing copyright regulations. Reference to these will be found in the Department of Education and Science's circular regarding the C.S.E. examinations.)

Another kind of test that is sometimes given in the C.S.E. is covered in part 9 below. This consists of a number of varied questions on a longer piece of music, the record or tape being played several times over, so that the pupil has a number of chances of listening to the music and sufficient time to supply written answers to the questions. Again, some suggestions are given here and the teacher can construct a number of similar questions on other records he happens to possess.

Some examinations ask candidates to recognise a well-known tune which is played below a counter-melody. This is a valuable test because it encourages pupils to hear the lower part of a texture. It is covered in part 10 below.

Finally, it is common practice to ask for the recognition of themes from the set works which have been studied. Suggestions with regard to this are given in part 11.

In all the examples which follow the answer to the questions is given in brackets.

1 Questions on instruments and orchestration

These questions may be concerned with the recognition of individual instruments; or they may ask about a group of instruments, the way they are used or with their grouping in an orchestra or band.

The teacher should look through all the records in his school library and decide which can be useful for these purposes. The examples given here are in alphabetical order of composers, so as to facilitate the finding of the relevant school records. If possible, the passages should then be transferred to tape, varying the kind of questions and their order as much as possible. Similar passages can be found by the teacher from other records he happens to possess.

(a) Individual instruments

This question may arise out of chamber music, e.g. Mozart's oboe quartet or clarinet quintet. The question may be asked: What wind instrument is used in addition to the string instruments?

Or it may arise out of a specific few bars in an orchestral record. The question will usually take the form: what instrument has the melody in these few bars?; though occasionally it may be a rhythm rather than a melody and the question will require adaptation, as is occasionally shown below.

BARTOK *Music for Strings, Percussion and Celesta.* What instrument starts the third movement? (Xylophone).

BEETHOVEN *Leonora Overture No.* 3. Bars 272–7 (Trumpet).
Symphony No. 2. Second movement. Bars 1–8 (Violin). 9–16 (Clarinet). Fourth movement. 98–104 (Bassoon).
Symphony No. 5. Third movement. Bars 19–26 (Horn).
Symphony No. 6. Second movement. What instruments provide the syncopated effect in bars 7–13? (Horns). Third movement. Bars 91–22 (Oboe).

122–33 (Clarinet). 133–4 (Horn). 165–80 (Violins). Fifth movement. Bars 1–5 (Clarinet). 5–9 (Horn). 9–16 (Violin).

Symphony No. 8. First movement. Bars 12–32 (Violin). Second movement. Bars 1–7 (Violin). Trio. Bars 1–4 (Horns). 5–8 (Clarinet).

BERLIOZ *Carnival Romaine.* Bars 21–37 (Cor Anglais).

BORODIN *Danses Polovtsiennes.* Introduction. Bars 15–23 (Oboe). 23–30 (Cor anglais). Second Dance. What instrument starts it in bars 1–4? (Timpani).

BRAHMS *Academic Festival Overture.* Bars 64–72 (Trumpet). 157–65 (Bassoon). 166–75 (Oboe).

Variations on a theme of Haydn. Variation VII. First 6 bars (Flute).

BRITTEN *Variations on a theme of Purcell.* Almost any variation between A and M can be used for this purpose, provided that the work is not already known and the record is not one which contains a spoken commentary (or the commentary is omitted from a tape, made from the record).

DEBUSSY *L'Après-midi d'un Faune.* Bars 1–4 (Flute).

DVORAK *New World Symphony.* First movement. Figure 5 for 8 bars (Flute). Second movement. Bars 7–18 (Cor anglais).

ELGAR *Enigma Variations.* Variation III. Figures 8–9 (Oboe). VI. Figures 19–22 (Viola). X. Figures 39–41 (Viola). XII. Figures 52–3 ('Cello). XIII Figures 56–7 (Clarinet)

HAYDN *Trumpet Concerto.* Second movement. Bars 9–16 (Trumpet).

Clock Symphony No. 101. Trio. First 12 bars (Flute).

Symphony No. 103. First movement. What instrument starts this symphony? (Drum). Second movement. Second variation of major theme, 135–42 (Oboes). Fourth movement. First four bars (Horn).

MENDELSSOHN *Hebrides Overture.* Bars 202–10 (Clarinet).

MOZART *Clarinet Concerto.* Second movement. Bars 1–8 (Clarinet).

Bassoon Concerto. Second movement. Bars 7–10 (Bassoon).

Quintet for piano, oboe, clarinet, horn and bassoon. K. 452. First movement. Bars 50³–54 (Piano). Third movement. Bars 1–8 (Piano). 9–16 (Oboe).

Symphony in E♭. K. 543. First section (Clarinets).

PROKOFIEV *Peter and the Wolf.* Almost any solo passage can be used, provided that the pupils do not already know it, and that parts containing the spoken voice are avoided.

RAVEL *Introduction and Allegro.* Figure 2–3 (Harp).

Bolero. Bar 5 up to Figure 1 (Flute). Figures 1–2 (Clarinet). Figures 2–3 (Bassoon). Figures 6–7 (Saxophone).

SCHUBERT *Trout Quintet.* Fourth movement. Variation I (Piano). Variation II (Viola). Variation V ('Cello).
Symphony No. 8. First movement. 42–54 ('Cello).

SCHUMANN *Piano Concerto.* Second movement. Bars 29–40 ('Cello).

STRAVINSKY *Soldier's Tale.* Music to Scene I. One bar after Figure 10—two bars after Figure 12 (Violin). Music to Scene II. Beginning as far as Figure 2 (Bassoon). Three bars before Figure 3 for 8 bars (Cornet). Royal March. First ten bars (Trombone).
Petrouchka. First 12 bars (Flute). Figures 22–23 (Clarinets). Figures 100–1 (Trumpets). Figures 104–6 (Cor anglais). Figures 125–7 (Clarinets). Figures 134–9 (Trumpet).

TSCHAIKOVSKY *Nutcracker Suite.* 'Dance of Sugar-Plum Fairy' (Celesta). 'Chinese Dance.' First 8 bars (Flute).
Swan Lake. I. Bars 1–19 (Oboe). II. Bars 19–50 (Violin).
Symphony No. 5 in *E minor.* Second movement. Bars 8–16 (Horn).

VAUGHAN WILLIAMS *Fantasia on a Theme of Tallis.* Bars 79–85 (Viola). Last 8 bars (Violin solo).

WAGNER *Overture to Tannhäuser.* Bars 38–53 (Trombone).
Siegfried Idyll. Bars 91–101 (Oboe). 148–60 (Clarinet). 259–74 (Horn).

WALTON *Façade. Swiss Jodelling Song.* First four bars (Bassoon).

WEBER *Overture to Der Freischütz.* Bars 10–25 (Horns).

If the teacher wishes he can add some examples from modern popular music, in which, perhaps, guitars, saxophones, drums, etc. are the solo instruments.

(b) Groups of instruments, or the way they are used

BACH *Brandenburg Concerto No.* 2. In the third movement the opening theme is played four times by different instruments, one after the other (bars 1–4). Name the instruments (Trumpet, oboe, violin, flute).
Brandenburg Concerto No. 5. In the first movement two instruments have a little duet (bars 9–19). Name them (Flute and violin).
Suite No. 2 *for Orchestra.* Name the two instruments playing in the overture bars 120–27 (Flute and violin).

BARTOK *Music for Strings, Percussion and Celesta.* First movement. The opening bars are played by strings. Are they playing pizzicato, arco or con sordino? (Con sordino). Second movement. Which way are the strings playing at 188–99? (Pizzicato). Is the drum playing single notes or a drum roll at (*i*) Bars 372–83? (Individual notes). (*ii*) Bars 385–92? (Roll). What effect is used by most of the strings at (*i*) 447–8? (Glissando). (*ii*) 450–8?

(Tremolo). Third movement. What are the three instruments you hear in addition to strings and drums at 35–43? (Celesta, harp and piano). Fourth movement. How are the strings playing at the beginning of the movement? (Pizzicato chords).

BEETHOVEN *Leonora Overture No.* 3. Bars 20–4. What two instruments are here playing in imitation? (Flute and violin). What instrument plays a short phrase twice underneath? (Bassoon).

Violin Concerto. First movement. What instrument starts the movement? (Timpani). What group plays next? (Wood-wind). After they have each played twice what group enters next? (Strings). Compare the opening bars with this entry (Each play repeated notes). How would you describe the passage at bars 18–24? (Ascending scales in wind). And how the passage at 28–35? (Tutti). What group of instruments play at bars 43–50? (Wind). And what group at 51–60? (Strings). Bars 284–301. What instrument is playing? (Violin). How would you describe this passage? (Cadenza). What kind of work is it likely to be part of? (Violin concerto).

Symphony No. 2. First movement. Bars 24–34. This is the end of an introduction. What is happening in the bass? (A pedal). Bars 73–6. What instruments play the tune? (Clarinet and bassoon). Bars 77–80. What instruments play the tune now? (Violins). Second movement. Bars 1–8. What group of instruments is playing? (Strings). To what group is the tune then transferred, 9–16? (Wind). Third movement. Trio. What group of instruments plays the first phrase? (Wind). And what the second after the repeat of the first phrase? (Strings). Fourth movement. Bars 358–65. Listen to the wind instruments and compare the first and second parts of the passage. (The notes they are playing are twice as long at the end of the passage (Augmentation).)

Symphony No. 5. First movement. Bars 59–62. What instrument starts this passage? (Horn). Who then has the tune? (Violins). And who next? (Clarinet). Second movement. What instruments play the theme at the beginning? (Viola and 'cello). Compare this with 50–7 (same instruments: a variant of the tune without the dotted notes); with 98–106 (same instru-, ments; notes twice as fast); and with 107–14 (moves to violins). Bars 127–43. What group of instruments play the tune? (Wood-wind). Third movement. Bars 320 to end of movement. Which cadence occurs in the first few bars? (Interrupted). Name the instrument which is used throughout the rest of the passage (Timpani). Name the instrument which plays a tune above it (Violin). What musical term describes such a passage? (*Crescendo*).

Symphony No. 6. Second movement. Bars 129–36 are meant to imitate birds. What instrument imitates the nightingale? (Flute). Which the quail? (Oboe). Which the cuckoo? (Clarinet). Third movement. Trio. Bars 90–122. What instrument plays the tune? (Oboe). What the accompaniment? (Violin). Bars 123–33. What instrument now plays the tune? (Clarinet). And what

I

the accompaniment? (Bassoon). Bars 133–45. What two instruments now play the tune in turn? (Horn and oboe). What group the accompaniment? (Strings). Can you hear another instrument present in this passage occasionally? (Bassoon). Fourth movement. Bars 21–3. This represents a storm Describe as fully as possible what instruments are used, to produce the effect (Wood-wind and brass loud chords; timpani, drum roll; upper strings, tremolo; lower strings, quick repeated scale passages). Bars 95–103 Describe what violin and 'cello are doing (Playing chromatic scales). What the rest of the strings are doing? (Tremolo chords).

Symphony No. 8. First movement. Bars 108–11. Listen to the passage several times. Four instruments are used here. Name the order in which they occur, and state the name given to this kind of writing (Bassoon, clarinet, oboe, flute. Imitation). Second movement. Bars 1–7. What instrument plays the tune? (Violin). Describe the accompaniment (Staccato repeated chords in wind and pizzicato strings). Third movement. Trio. What instruments play the first phrase? (Horns). And what the second? (Clarinet).

BORODIN *Danses Polovtsiennes.* Introduction. Which two instruments open this movement with a duet? (Flute and oboe).

BRAHMS *Variations on a theme of Haydn.* Theme. Two kinds of instruments open with the theme. What are they? (Oboe and bassoon).
Variation VII. What two instruments open with the theme here? (Flute and viola).

DVORAK *Carnival Overture.* Bars 132–8. What percussion instruments can you hear? (Tambourine and triangle). Bars 161–6. What percussion instrument is added here? (Cymbals). Bars 218–30. What string instruments are playing and what device are they using? (Violin and viola, con sordini). What instrument plays a short, repeated accompaniment? (Cor anglais). What instrument starts the tune? (Flute). And what instrument joins in with the tune two bars later? (Oboe).

New World Symphony. First movement. Beginning of allegro. What instruments have the first phrase? (Horns). And what the answering phrase? (Clarinet and bassoons). Figure 7. Compare the use of the trumpet and the violin (Trumpet plays the same theme as the violin more slowly; augmentation). Second movement. What is the main group of instruments heard in bars 1–4? (Brass). And in 5–6, and how are they playing? (Muted strings). Third movement. Trio. What group of instruments starts the trio? (Wood-wind). And what group continues after the repeat? (Strings).

ELGAR *Cockaigne Overture.* This is a picture of London Town. What would you say was passing through the street at Figures 17–18 and why? (A band, because of the cornets and trombones).
Enigma Variations. Dorabella. What method of playing are the violins using throughout this number (Muted). And what method the lower strings, most

of the time? (Muted pizzicato). What instrument plays the tune, from Figure 39–40? (Viola).

HAYDN *Symphony No.* 99 *in E♭.* Second movement. Bars 16–27. Name the three instruments playing. (Flute, oboe and bassoon).
   Symphony No. 101. *The Clock.* Trio. Which instruments play the accompaniment, at first? (Strings). What instrument mostly plays the tune, in the first half? (Flute). The second part of the trio starts with a duet between two instruments. Which two? (Flute and bassoon).

RAVEL *Introduction and Allegro.* What device does the harp use twice between Figures 6 and 8? (Chord glissandos). What instrument is playing from ten bars after Figure 17 up to Figure 18? (Harp). How would you describe this passage? (Cadenza). Name the two devices used by this instrument during this passage. (Glissandos and harmonics).

SMETANA *Overture to the Bartered Bride.* Bars 14–80. How would you describe this passage? (Strings, using imitations).

STRAVINSKY *Soldier's Tale.* Music to Scene 1. What two instruments start this movement? (Violin and double bass). The little concert. What three instruments are playing from Figure 28 to the end? (Clarinet, cornet and violin). Waltz. What three instruments are playing from Figures 10 to 12? (Bassoon, violin and double bass).

TSCHAIKOVSKY *Nutcracker Suite.* March. What group of instruments starts the march? (Wind). What group comes next? (Strings).
   Symphony No. 4. Third movement. What group of instruments starts this movement, and how do they play? (Strings, pizzicato). Who play the next section? (Wind).

   All the above examples are from well-known classics. If the teacher wishes to include some modern jazz or popular music, he can quite well do so.

2 Recognition of type of voice or of particular singer

   The best preparation for this type of question is to tell the class the name of of the singer, and the type of voice he or she has, every time they listen to a record which includes vocal soloists.
   They should become familiar with the particular type of vocal quality that a soprano, contralto, tenor or bass possesses, so that they judge by this quality rather than by vocal range which can, at times, be very deceptive. For this reason a mezzo-soprano, a dramatic soprano with a very wide range, or a baritone with a tenor or bass vocal quality can be difficult to 'place'; and it would be unreasonable to expect a correct answer from the type of candidate for whom this C.S.E. type of question is designed.
   So, to be fair, the test should present a light or high coloratura soprano, a contralto with really deep, dark tones in her voice, a lyrical tenor with the

tone quality associated with tenor high notes or a deep, powerful bass. A boy's treble voice should also be recognisable.

This is, therefore, a simple type of question that does not need to be asked very often. It must necessarily be based on the vocal records that the teacher or the school possesses. And it is perhaps best linked with a series of other questions, as is suggested in part 9 below.

Occasionally the name of a particular singer could reasonably be asked for, perhaps by supplying a further piece of information that should help with the identification.

For example:

(*a*) Here is a famous Australian singer who is well-known for her portrayal of Italian operatic parts. What is her name? (An Italian operatic aria sung by Joan Sutherland.)

(*b*) This singer is famous as a lieder singer. What is her name? (Elizabeth Schwarzkopf singing in German.)

(*c*) This English contralto is well-known as an oratorio singer and a lieder singer. What is her name? (Janet Baker singing an aria from an oratorio or a Purcell song.)

(*d*) This singer is particularly associated with Benjamin Britten. What is his name? (Peter Pears singing in some work by Britten.)

(*e*) This singer is famous as a lieder singer. What is his name? (Dietrich Fischer-Dieskau singing in German.)

(*f*) What instrument do you associate with this voice? (Louis Armstrong and the trumpet.) (This question has been set by the Department of Education and Science as an example for C.S.E.)

(*g*) A question on any singer who is currently popular as a jazz, folk or 'pop' singer. (The song should be one for which he or she is well-known, accompanied by the instruments usually associated with him or her.) (Fashions change so quickly in this kind of music that it is unwise to suggest a particular song or singer, in this instance.)

3 Recognition of type of Vocal Composition or a Particular Vocal Work

This type of question will again have to be based on the records possessed by the teacher or the school. It can often take the form of a choice of alternatives.

For example:

(*a*) Is this a part song, a chorus or a madrigal? (A question set by the Department of Education and Science as a C.S.E. question.)

(*b*) Is this an operatic chorus or a chorus from an oratorio?

(*c*) Is this a folk song or an art song?

(*d*) Is this a glee or a part song (i.e. Is it for male voices only or for mixed voices?).

(*e*) Is this a motet or an anthem (i.e. Is it sung in Latin or English?).

(*f*) Is this an operatic aria or an aria from an oratorio? (The words are the main clue here.)

(*g*) Is this a recitative or an aria? (The example given should be clearly one or the other, and not the arioso type.)

(*h*) What name is given to this type of composition? (A fugue.)

(*i*) What kind of negro song is this? (A negro spiritual or Blues.)

Alternatively a question might be given on the recognition of a particular vocal work, provided that it was well-known.

For example:

(*a*) Here is a song by Schubert sung in German. What is the title usually given to it in English? (Possible examples could be *The Erl King, Who is Sylvia, Hark, hark the lark, The Trout, Hedge Rose*.)

(*b*) This chorus comes from a well-known oratorio. What is the name of the oratorio? (Any well-known chorus from *The Messiah* or *Elijah*.)

(*c*) This aria comes from a well-known oratorio. What is the name of the oratorio? (Any well-known aria from *The Messiah, The Creation* or *Elijah*.)

(*d*) This aria (or duet) comes from a well-known opera. What is the name of the opera? (Any well-known aria (or duet) from a Mozart, Verdi or Gilbert and Sullivan opera.)

(*e*) This song comes from a well-known 'musical'. What is the name of the musical? (Any currently popular music.)

4 Recognition of type of chamber group

Pupils must know the names of the instruments which comprise all the well-known groups, such as: violin, 'cello, flute or clarinet sonata; piano, or string or clarinet trio; piano, string, oboe or clarinet quartet; piano, string or clarinet quintet; string sextet. They must also learn to recognise the sound of each instrument and be able to tell how many instruments are playing.

The question might take the form of:

(*a*) Name the group of instruments playing in this extract (string quartet or clarinet trio).

(*b*) Is this an oboe, clarinet or piano quintet?

(*c*) Tell the pupils the names of three (or four) instruments playing in an extract and ask for the fourth (or fifth).

(*d*) Ask for the names of two (or three) instruments playing in a duet (or trio).

Particular examples must perforce be taken from those in the school's or the teacher's library.

5 Recognition of a large instrumental group, or section of it, or of a particular movement from it

Questions could be asked on whether a work was played by a symphony orchestra, a brass band or a military band; or whether it was a concerto and, if so, for what instrument.

Questions might also be asked on which section of a symphony orchestra was playing (string, wood-wind, brass or percussion). Or it might be a combination of two of them. Alternatively they might be asked which section was *not* playing.

They could also be asked whether a particular movement in a symphony was the first, second or third. (First and fourth movements could easily be confused; but a slow movement, a minuet and trio or a scherzo and trio should be recognisable and easily distinguished from an *allegro* or *vivace*, which could be a first or last movement.

Pupils could also be asked to identify a type of concerto and perhaps to suggest a performer who might play it.

Questions must again be based on the particular records available.

6 Recognition of form, structure or modulation

The examples chosen should be in a clearly-defined form and preferably not too long. For example, a movement in sonata form is unlikely to be set in a group of short questions, as it would take at least three or four minutes to hear.

Possible examples:

(*a*) A movement from a classical suite, which is obviously in binary form.

(*b*) A movement which is in a clearly-defined ternary form. It may be as short as *Charlie is my darling*; or it may be a modern piano piece on the plan A B A.

(*c*) A movement in rondo form. It may be by Couperin, or be a song such as Purcell's *I attempt from Love's Sickness to fly*. It should not be in sonata-rondo form; and most true rondos in a sonata or symphony will probably be too long for the purpose, though the finale from Beethoven's piano sonata, *Op.* 79, is possible.

(*d*) A movement in variation form. The teacher will probably find he has plenty of examples in his collection of records. He may play the *andante* from Beethoven's piano sonata, *Op.* 14 *No.* 2, on the piano himself, or Schubert's *Impromptu in B flat*. He will find plenty of examples by Haydn—the slow movement of the string quartet, *Op.* 76 *No.* 3, based on the Emperor's hymn is perhaps the best-known. Another easily recognised example is the variation movement from Schubert's *Trout quintet*, though this is rather long. The more modern type of variation, in which the theme undergoes considerable metamorphosis, such as Brahms' *Variations on a theme of Haydn* or Elgar's *Enigma Variations* is too difficult for this purpose.

(*e*) A ground bass. There are four examples in Purcell's *Dido and Aeneas*, the most famous being 'When I am laid in Earth'. The finale of Brahms' *Variations on a theme of Haydn* is possible, as is the finale of Beethoven's *Eroica symphony* and the finale of Brahms' *Fourth symphony*, though these are rather long for this purpose.

(*f*) A short movement in fugue form.

Particular questions on the structure of a piece are also possible. The pupil may be asked how many times a particular theme appears; to recognise a theme when it reappears in the bass; to recognise a sequence or a particular modulation, an example of augmentation or diminution. These latter may require the students to possess a copy, so that they can mark the particular device or name the bar number where it occurs. Alternatively, to save time, a class can put their hands up when they hear it.

Another way of dealing with this type of question is to give a short extract and ask what device is used in it. It may be an example of imitation, sequence, augmentation or diminution; or they may be told the key of a piece and asked what key it has reached at the end of the extract (which should be the dominant major or the relative major or minor in a C.S.E. question). This will probably require isolating on tape, from a longer piece of music; and once more, it will depend upon the particular records available.

7 Recognition of dance forms

The students should learn the characteristic rhythms of the dances of the classical composers, such as minuets, gavottes, bourrées, passepieds, gigues; of the nineteenth composers, such as waltzes, polkas, polonaises, mazurkas, seguidillas; and of the twentieth century, such as fox-trots, tangos and rumbas. (A definition of most of these will be found in Section 15 of the author's *Basic Music Knowledge*.) He should hear as many as possible, in order to become familiar with the sound. Then extracts should be played from examples not previously heard, for the candidates to identify the type of dance.

Sometimes the orchestration will help to identify the dance. And sometimes the question can take the form of asking which of three or four dances of contrasting nature the dance is.

8 Recognition of period

The pupils should have heard a good deal of music of different periods before such questions are set. The harmony, the scoring, the texture, and the rhythms used all help in this identification.

But comparisons of composers of the same period should not be attempted. Much of Bach and Handel, Haydn and Mozart, or Chopin and Mendelssohn can sound alike to a pupil at the C.S.E. stage. The comparison should be between well-contrasted composers.

For example:

(*a*) Is this music by *i*. Byrd, Chopin or Bartok? *ii*. Bach, Beethoven or Schönberg? *iii*. Handel, Schumann or Stravinsky?

(*b*) Is this music classical, romantic, serial, electronic or modern popular?

(*c*) Do you think this music was written in the sixteenth, eighteenth or twentieth century?

9 Answering a number of varied questions on a piece of music, after several hearings of it

The students should be given a list of written questions and should have time to read them before the record starts. The record should be repeated several times, with about half-a-minute's interval between each time; and the students should write their answers in the spaces provided at any time they wish.

The preparation for all the likely questions has already been given in earlier parts of this book and, in particular, in the earlier parts of this Section. So the only new difficulty is learning to hear and attend to several different things at the same time. The pupils will need practice in this. The questions must again be based on the records available. But specimen questions on each kind of music are given here, and they are based on records that schools are likely to possess. The teacher can make up further lists of questions on similar works, if necessary.

(a) Solo Vocal Works (Folk Songs)

This kind of work is the easiest kind to answer questions upon, as the words are so helpful – provided they can be clearly heard – and they also encourage the pupils to listen more keenly.

The Flowers in the Valley
1. How many knights came courting? (Three.)
2. What colours did they wear? (Red, green and yellow.)
3. What colour did the man wear who was successful? (Yellow.)

Dashing away with the Smoothing Iron
What did the girl do with her linen each day of the week? Monday? (Washing); Tuesday? (Hanging out); Wednesday? (Starching); Thursday? (Ironing); Friday? (Folding); Saturday? (Airing); Sunday? (Wearing).

These kind of questions are simply designed to focus the pupils' attention. They can, if wished, be combined with questions on the time, a suitable speed mark, and asking for letters A, B, etc., describing the shape of the tune, where appropriate.

(b) Solo Vocal Works (Art Songs)

ARNE *When Daisies pied*
1. The key of this song is F major. In what key is it at 'do paint the meadows with delight'? (C major.)
2. What device is used at 'mocks married men'? (Sequences.)
3. What device is used for the repeated 'Cuckoo'? (Imitation.)
4. Would you say the speed mark was *vivace*, *allegretto* or *largo*? (*Allegretto*.)
5. Is it in $\frac{2}{4}$, $\frac{3}{4}$ or $\frac{4}{4}$ time? ($\frac{3}{4}$)

BRAHMS *Der Schmied* (*The Blacksmith*)
1. Name two ways which you think convey the impression of the blacksmith and his forge? (The quick syncopated figure (♪ 𝄽) in the accom-

232

paniment, suggesting the quick blows; and the large leaps in the voice part suggesting the big swing of the hammer.)

2. Nearly all the notes in the voice part are the same length. Assuming that the time signature is $\frac{3}{4}$, what is this length? (Crotchet.)

3. Which two of the following do you think are used in this song? *Allegro; lento; piano; forte*? (*Allegro* and *forte*.)

GRIEG *Solveig's Song*

1. Is this song in a major or a minor key? (Minor.)

2. What device is used at the end of each verse? (Coloratura.)

3. Would you say the accompaniment was harmonic or contrapuntal? (Harmonic.)

4. Would you say the speed mark was *un poco andante, presto con fuoco,* or *largo grandioso*? (*Un poco andante.*)

5. Is it in simple or compound time? (Simple.)

6. Is this song by a sixteenth, seventeenth or nineteenth century composer? (Nineteenth century.)

7. Give his name, if known. (Grieg.)

MENDELSSOHN *On Wings of Song*

1. Is this song in simple or compound time? (Compound.)

2. There are three verses. Which two are the same? (The first and second.)

3. What device is used at the end of the song? (Coda.)

4. Would you say it was legato or staccato? (Legato.)

5. Is it *allegro giocoso* or *andante tranquillo*? (*Andante tranquillo*.)

6. Is this song by a romantic, classical or modern composer? (Romantic.)

7. Give his name, if you know it. (Mendelssohn.)

SCHUBERT *Hark, Hark the lark*

1. Who wrote the words of this song? (Shakespeare.)

2. Translate 'pretty bin' into modern English. (Pretty is.)

3. Is this song in simple or compound time? (Compound.)

4. How does the composer treat the word 'arise'? (Leaps up to it, and repeats it, falling each time.)

5. How often is the lady told to arise? (Eight times.)

6. Is the composer Bach, Schubert, or Britten? (Schubert.)

Gute Nacht (*Good Night*) *No.* 1 *of Winterreise*

1. How many verses are there in this song? (Four.)

2. What is the main difference between the last verse and the others? (It is in the major while the others are in the minor.)

3. How would you describe the accompaniment? (Mostly repeated chords.)

4. Is it in $\frac{2}{4}$, $\frac{3}{4}$ or $\frac{4}{4}$ time? ($\frac{2}{4}$ time.)

5. Compare the first and second phrase of each verse. (They are the same.)

The Erl King (assuming it is sung in English).

1. Who wrote the original German words of this song? (Goethe.)
2. What does the accompaniment represent? (The galloping horse.)
3. How many people speak in the song and who are they? (Three: the father, the son and the Erl King.)
4. What device is used at the end of the song? (Recitative.)
5. Is this song in repeated stanzas or *durchcomponiert*? (*Durchcomponiert.*)

(c) Opera

GILBERT AND SULLIVAN *The Mikado Act I, No. 5. Behold the Lord High Executioner*

1. What instruments play the introduction? (Brass.)
2. Two types of voice start singing the chorus. What are they? (Tenor and bass.)
3. Are they singing in unison or two parts at first? (Unison.)
4. Do they continue like this throughout the opening chorus? If not, what change takes place? (They sing in three parts, on two occasions.)
5. What kind of voice has the soloist? (Baritone.)
6. Would you say he was singing coloratura, cantabile or parlando? (Parlando.)
7. When the chorus re-enters, what is its relationship to the solo voice? (It is in imitation.)
8. How many parts are there in it now? (Four.)
9. How does the number end? (It uses the second section of the opening chorus.)
10. How many different voice-parts are heard at the end? (Four.)
11. Name the composer, if you know it. (Sullivan.)

MOZART *The Magic Flute. Sarastro's aria at the beginning of Act II*

1. What kind of voice takes the solo part? (Bass.)
2. What kind of voices are used in the chorus at the end of each half? (Tenors and Basses.)
3. Name the instruments which stand out in the accompaniment? (Trombones.)
4. What instruments usually prominent in an orchestra are absent from this number? (Violins.)
5. Is this number in duple, triple or quadriple time? (Triple.)
6. Is the speed *presto, moderato* or *adagio*? (*Adagio.*)
7. Is it by Handel, Mozart or Verdi? (Mozart.)

VERDI *Rigoletto. Caro Nome*

1. What word describes the introduction to this aria? (Recitative.)
2. What kind of voice sings this aria? (Soprano.)
3. Is the first phrase of the aria legato or staccato? (Staccato.)
4. What effect joins the first to the second phrase? (Portamento.)

5. Compare the second phrase with the first. (Sequence, a note lower.)

6. As the aria reaches its climax what device does the singer use? (Coloratura.)

7. How does the aria end? (With a quiet return to the opening theme.)

8. Describe the accompaniment to the last phrases. (The orchestra plays the original phrase in syncopation, later followed by high tremolo violins and pizzicato bass.)

9. Do you think this aria is by a seventeenth, eighteenth or nineteenth century composer? (Nineteenth century.)

(d) Cantata and oratorio

BACH *Sleepers, Wake!*

1. In the first chorus there is a German hymn tune present. What is the name for a German hymn tune? (Chorale.)

2. What voice sings it? (Treble.)

3. Does it move more slowly or more quickly than the other parts? (More slowly.)

4. What device is used to describe the entrance of the other voices? (Imitative entries.)

5. What particular feature is present in the orchestral part at the beginning? (Dotted notes.)

6. Do you think that the composer was Bach, Beethoven or Britten? (Bach.)

7. What voices sing the hymn tune in No. 4? (Tenors.)

8. There is a counter-theme in No. 4. What instruments play it? (Violins and violas in unison.)

9. How is the hymn tune treated in No. 9? (Four part choir: soprano, alto, tenor and bass.)

10. Do you know the name of the hymn tune in English? ('Sleepers Wake,' or 'Wake, O wake, for Night is flying.')

11. This work has nine numbers; and the other numbers are solos or duets. What word describes this kind of work? (Cantata.)

HANDEL *The Messiah. For unto us a Child is born*

1. What voice enters first in this chorus? (Soprano.)

2. What voice enters second in this chorus? (Tenor.)

3. How would you describe it in relation to the first? (Imitation, an octave lower.)

4. What voice enters next? (Alto.)

5. And what next? (Bass.)

6. What term describes the runs on the word 'born'? (Coloratura.)

7. Describe the use of the voices at 'And the government shall be upon His shoulder'. (Dotted notes and imitative entries.)

8. Compare this with the words 'Wonderful. Counsellor, the mighty God'. (All the voices enter together in harmony.)

9. Name the composer and the work from which this chorus is taken (Handel, *The Messiah*.)

10. What kind of a work is it? (An oratorio.)

HAYDN *The Creation. And God made the Firmament*

1. What kind of voice sings this number? (Bass.)

2. What term is used to describe the first few bars of the voice part? ('Recitativo secco' or 'dry recitative.')

3. What term is used to describe it later? ('Recitativo accompagnato' or 'accompanied recitative.')

4. The accompaniment from here to the end is descriptive. Do the descriptions come before or after the words which describe them? (Before.)

5. How is the snow described in music? (By gentle, very short chords, with the top part syncopated.)

The Creation. With Verdure clad

1. What kind of voice sings this number? (Soprano.)

2. Mention two words on which coloratura is used. (Enhanced; plant).

3. In what form is this aria? (Ternary.)

4. Is there a coda? (Yes.)

5. What time signature do you think is used for this aria? ($\frac{6}{8}$)

6. Name the composer and the work from which this and the previous number was taken. (Haydn, *The Creation*.)

MENDELSSOHN *Elijah. The last Baal chorus*

1. What word best describes the speed of this number: *moderato, presto andante*? (*Presto*.)

2. Describe the string parts in the first few bars. (Quick scales.)

3. There are four voice-parts. When they first sing together at 'Hear and answer, Baal' are they singing in four different parts? (No. they are singing in unison.)

4. How do they continue at 'Mark how the scorner derideth us?' (Imitative entries.)

5. What are the upper strings doing at this stage? (Tremolo.)

6. Are the brass and percussion playing at this stage? (Yes.)

7. When 'Mark how the scorner derideth us' appears for the last time describe the soprano part. (It descends by step.)

8. After this, and towards the end of the chorus, how is 'Hear and answer' made to stand out? (By means of dramatic pauses, waiting for the answer.)

9. Name the composer and the title of the work. (Mendelssohn, *Elijah*.)

(e) Chamber music

HAYDN *String Quartet in D minor, Op.* 76, *No.* 2. *Third movement*

1. Name the instruments used in this work. (Two violins, viola and 'cello.)

2. State what this combination is called. (String quartet).

3. Listen to the two highest instruments in the minuet. What do you notice about them? (They are playing in octaves.)

4. Listen to the two lowest instruments in the minuet. State *two* things you notice about them. (They are in octaves and are playing in canon with the two highest instruments a bar later).

5. Does the opening of the minuet return later? (Yes.)

6. Is the minuet in a major or a minor key? (Minor.)

7. Is the trio in a major or a minor key? (Major.)

8. What relationship has this key to the key of the minuet? (Tonic major.)

9. Does the trio modulate, and if so to what related key and at what place? (To the dominant at the end of the first half.)

10. In the trio what is a feature of the bass part most of the time? (It has pedals, mostly on tonic and dominant.)

11. Do you think the composer is Haydn, Brahms or Bartok? (Haydn.)

Emperor Quartet, Op. 76, *No.* 3. *Second movement*

1. This movement is a theme with variations. Listen to the theme and identify it, if possible. (Emperor's Hymn; Austrian National Anthem; Praise the Lord, ye heavens adore Him; Glorious Things of Thee are spoken, or hymn tune).

2. Two instruments play the first variation. Which are they, and what do they do? (Both violins. One plays the theme, and the other plays a quicker counter-theme round it.)

3. Who has the theme in Variation II? ('Cello.)

4. Who has the theme in Variation III? (Viola.)

5. There are two main ways in which variation IV differs from the theme, What are they? (The harmonies are different; and from the second phrase to the end the theme is an octave higher.)

6. Name the composer. (Haydn).

MOZART *Clarinet Quintet. Last movement. Theme and first variation*

1. This movement is for string quartet plus one other instrument. What is this other instrument? (Clarinet.)

2. This movement is a theme with variations. You are to hear the theme and the first variation. By means of letters describe the plan of the theme (AA:‖BA:).

3. Who has the main tune in the theme? (First violin.)

4. In the second half of the theme what instrument imitates it in the first few bars? (Viola.)

5. In the first variation what instrument has the first phrase of the theme? (Violin.)

6. What instrument has a counter-theme above it? (Clarinet.)

7. What instrument starts the second phrase of the theme? (Viola.)

8. What instrument has a decorated version of the theme at the beginning of the second half of this variation? (Clarinet.)

9. What instrument returns to the original version of the theme at the end of this variation? (Violin.)

10. Is the composer Mozart, Brahms or Debussy? (Mozart.)

(f) Concertos

BEETHOVEN *Piano Concerto No. 3 in C minor. Third movement, bars* 1–55

1. What kind of a work is this extract taken from? (Piano concerto.)

2. Which movement is it likely to be? (The third.)

3. What instrument opens with the first theme? (Piano.)

4. What instrument has this theme next? (Oboe.)

5. What is the first instrument doing at the same time? (Playing quick passage work, semiquavers.)

6. What instrument has the second theme? (Piano.)

7. How do you describe the short passage which leads to the return of the first theme? (Cadenza.)

8. Who plays this return of the first theme? (Piano.)

9. When the second theme returns who play it and continue to the end of the extract? (All the orchestra; *tutti*.)

10. Is the composer Beethoven, Liszt or Rachmaninov? (Beethoven.)

HAYDN *Trumpet Concerto. Finale, bars* 1–68

1. The first theme is played three times, in this extract. Who play it the first time? (Violins.)

2. Who play it the second time? (A *tutti*, the theme played by flutes, violins and bassoons.)

3. Who plays it the third time? (Trumpet.)

4. Write down the rhythm of the first phrase (four bars) of the tune, complete with time signature and speed mark. (*Allegro* $\frac{2}{4}$ ♩. ♪|♩. ♪|♫♫|♩ ‖.)

5. What kind of a work do you think this is? (A trumpet concerto.)

6. Does the composer belong to the eighteenth or the twentieth century? (Eighteenth.)

MENDELSSOHN *Violin Concerto. Second movement*

1. What kind of a work is this movement taken from? (Violin concerto.)

2. Which movement of the work is it? (The second, the slow movement.)

3. Is it in simple or compound time? (Compound.)

4. Is it *allegro, andante* or *largo*? (*Andante*.)

5. What instrument plays the first melody? (Violin.)

6. What instruments play the accompaniment to this melody? Describe this accompaniment. (Strings. Broken chords.)

7. What happens at the end of this first melody? (All the orchestra plays: a *tutti*.)

8. Describe the second melody which the soloist introduces. What device is being used? (A melody, with accompanying broken chords underneath, producing double stopping.)

9. In what form is this movement as a whole? (Ternary.)

10. Are the timpani present in this movement; and, if so, where are they used? (Yes. The middle section.)

MOZART *Bassoon Concerto in B flat major, K.191. First movement, bars* 1–71 (*Exposition*)

1. Name as many instruments as you can that you hear in the first part of this extract. (Oboes, bassoon, horns and strings.)

2. What instruments play the first theme the first time? (Violins.)

3. Upon what chord are the first two bars used? (Tonic chord, I.)

4. Upon what chord is the third bar based? (Dominant chord, V.)

5. Upon what chord is the fourth bar based? (Tonic chord, I.)

6. What instruments play the second theme which appears at bar 11? Describe how it starts. (Violins. Broken chords.)

7. About halfway through this extract a soloist enters. What instrument is he playing? (Bassoon.)

8. What theme does he play at first? (The first theme, repeated.)

9. When the second theme returns what are the two main differences between this and its first appearance? (It was in the tonic key and is now in the dominant key. Also the bassoon is now playing a counter-theme.)

10. This extract is only part of a movement. What names are likely to be given to the first two themes you have heard? (First and second subjects.)

11. What type of a work is this? (A bassoon concerto.)

12. Which movement is this likely to be? (The first movement.)

13. What part of the movement do you think you have heard? (The exposition, repeated when the soloist enters.)

14. The soloist plays many quick, semiquaver passages. What other features do you notice about his part? (Big leaps.)

15. In what century do you think this work was written? (Eighteenth.)

(g) *Orchestral works, other than concertos*

BEETHOVEN *Egmont Overture. Bars* 1–66

1. The beginning of this extract is marked with two of the following: *presto con fuoco; sostenuto ma non troppo; marcato; cantabile*. Which two? (*Sostenuto ma non troppo; marcato*.)

2. What family of instruments plays the first phrase? (String family.)

3. What family of instruments plays the second phrase? (Wood-wind.)

4. What device is this second family using? (Imitation.)

5. A short phrase with the melody in the violin then follows. What happens after this? (A repetition of the first phrase, *ff, tutti*.)

6. What happens next? (Wood-wind imitations again.)

7. A short figure for violin follows, which is frequently repeated. It is doubled by three different instruments in turn. Name them in order of appearance. (Clarinet; flute (also bassoon, which may not be heard); oboe.)

8. The speed then changes to *allegro*. Compare the first few bars of the *allegro* with the preceding figure mentioned in question 7. (It is the same but quicker.)

9. What instrument has the melody a few bars later? ('Cello.)

10. What instrument joins in at the end of the first two phrases of this melody? (Violin.)

11. Describe what is happening in the last few bars of the extract, stating the theme, who is playing it and with what dynamics (The theme from the beginning of the *allegro*, played by the violins in a *forte tutti*).

12. What name is given to the first slow part of this extract? (Introduction.)

13. Is the composer Mozart, Beethoven or Mendelssohn? (Beethoven.)

BRAHMS *Variations on a theme of Haydn. Variation IV*

1. The beginning of this extract is marked with three of the following: *con moto; allegro vivace; largo e mesto; f; p; staccato; dolce e semplice.* Which three? (*Con moto; p; dolce e semplice.*)

2. What two instruments have the theme in the first five-bar phrase? (Oboe and horn.)

3. What additional two instruments join in at bar 6? (Flute and bassoon.)

4. Who has both phrases of this melody when it is repeated? (Violins and violas.)

5. Which instruments have a quicker-moving accompaniment at the same time? (Wood-wind.)

6. Compare the scoring of the second half of this whole extract with that of the first. (It is exactly the same.)

7. Is it by Handel, Brahms or Stravinsky? (Brahms.)

HAYDN *Symphony No. 99 in E flat. Finale. Bars 1–20*

1. What family of instruments play the first sentence? (String family.)

2. What instrument do you hear playing two notes at the end of this sentence? (Horn.)

3. Listen to the tune at the beginning. What instruments start it when it returns later? ('Cellos and basses.)

4. At this stage three sets of instruments have it in turn. What device is this called? (Imitation.)

5. This is the beginning of a movement of a symphony. Is it likely to be the first, second, third or fourth? (Fourth.)

6. Is the work by Haydn, Brahms or Elgar? (Haydn.)

MENDELSSOHN *Hebrides Overture. Bars 1–26*

1. The opening one-bar figure is played twice by three instruments. What are they? (Bassoons, violas and 'cellos.)

2. It is then repeated twice. How much higher or lower? (A third higher.)

3. It is then repeated twice more. How much higher or lower? (A third higher again.)

4. What is this kind of device called? (A sequence.)

5. A few bars later it is repeated again. By what instruments? (Violins.)

6. A new phrase is then heard twice in the violins, followed by a *tutti*. What percussion instrument do you hear in this *tutti*? (Drum roll.)

7. How many times do you hear this percussion effect from here to the end of the extract? (Three times.)

8. Name the work, if you know it. (*Hebrides Overture;* or *Fingal's Cave.*)

MOZART *Symphony in E flat, K.543. Trio*

1. What instrument plays the first two phrases of the tune. (Clarinet.)

2. What instrument provides a broken-chord accompaniment to it? (A second clarinet.)

3. What instrument imitates the tune at the end of each of these phrases? (Flute.)

4. After all this is repeated what instrument has the tune next? (Violin.)

5. What pair of instruments joins this phrase to a repetition of the beginning? (Trumpets.)

6. Is this movement in duple, triple or quadruple time? (Triple.)

7. Would you say it was lightly or heavily scored? (Lightly.)

8. This movement is part of a symphony. Which part? (Trio.)

9. Is this symphony by Mozart, Beethoven or Brahms? (Mozart.)

STRAVINSKY *Petrouchka. Valse. Figures* 140–8

1. What instrument starts thus extract? (Bassoon.)

2. What instrument starts a melody in the fifth bar? (Trumpet.)

3. What instrument takes up the melody a bar later? (Flute.)

4. These three instruments continue until there is a pause. Then two instruments start to play together. What are they? (Flutes and harp.)

5. Is the tune duple, triple or quadruple up to here? (Triple.)

6. After eight bars of these two instruments two more enter, and continue against the first two for some time. What are they? (Cor anglais and double bassoon.)

7. Are they playing in duple, triple or quadruple time? (Duple.)

8. What device do the two pairs of instruments produce? (Cross rhythm.)

9. There are four interruptions by another instrument. Which? (Trumpet.)

10. What instruments provide an occasional bass and how do they play? ('Cello and bass pizzicato.)

11. Which of the four instruments are left to themselves at the end of the extract? (Cor anglais and bassoon.)

12. This number has the title of a dance. What dance? (Valse.)

TSCHAIKOVSKY *Casse Noisette Suite. March*

1. What families of instruments play the first phrase? (Wood-wind and brass.)

2. And what the second? (Strings.)

3. After all this has been repeated, who plays next? (Trumpets and trombones.)

4. How do the strings play in the next phrase? (Pizzicato.)

5. Name a percussion instrument which is heard occasionally. (Cymbals.)

6. Is the time of this extract duple, triple or quadruple? (Quadruple.)

7. Suggest a title concerned with its rhythm. (March.)

8. What is the form of this extract? (Ternary.)

9. Do you think it is by a sixteenth or nineteenth century composer? (Nineteenth.)

10. Name the composer and the work, if you know them. (Tschaikovsky, *Casse noisette* or *Nutcracker Suite*.)

10 Recognition of a hidden melody

Composers quite often repeat a melody in the middle or at the bottom of the texture; and some students miss the enjoyment of its re-appearance because they cannot hear a lower tune with counter-melodies or harmonies above it. Practice in recognising lower melodies is therefore very useful.

Of course, a composer often has a melody played by the 'cellos or the trombones which is quite easy to hear, either because it is unaccompanied or its accompaniment is so light or so different that the melody easily comes through. Such melodies as that played by the 'cellos at the beginning of the second subject in the first movement of Schubert's *Unfinished Symphony* or the trombones in Wagner's *Tannhäuser Overture* are cases in point. But at other times the recognition of a lower melody does present difficulty.

There are two main methods of giving practice in acquiring this most valuable aural ability. One is to make use of existing classics, letting the pupils hear the original melody and asking them to recognise is on its later appearance; and the other is to construct examples with a well-known melody underneath and ask for its recognition. Examples of both methods are given here.

(a) Recognition of a melody when it appears below other melodies or harmonies in a classical composition

The simplest way of dealing with this question is to let a class hear the original melody and then ask for a show of hands every time it reappears.

The teacher who is a good pianist can play any suitable Bach fugue and ask for the recognition of the subject in this way. In some cases it may be possible for the class to write down the number of times it appears, perhaps in only part of the fugue.

Bach is a particularly useful composer for this purpose because it is more difficult to hear a lower melody which is part of a contrapuntal texture. Accordingly a number of Bach examples are suggested here. But the examples are in alphabetical order of composers so that teachers can more easily check with records they happen to possess and can make use of. They are, therefore, not in order of difficulty.

Suggestions are given below as to the best way of giving each test, but the teacher can adapt them as he wishes. He may play the whole movement or he may isolate the particular passage. In the latter case it will often be worth while to put the test on tape.

BACH *Violin Concerto in E major. Slow movement*
This is a *basso ostinato*. The bass is clearly heard the first time, and the students should listen to it carefully. It is six bars long. They might then listen to the whole movement and be asked how many times they have heard a more-or-less complete statement or development of it in the bass. Partial entries of only a bar or so should not be counted. (Seven times.)

Concerto for two Violins in D minor. First movement
This is a fugue. The class would enjoy the whole movement, but they might be asked to listen to the subject in the first four bars and then to recognise its entry in the bass at bar 10.

Brandenburg Concerto No. 1. Slow movement
The class should listen to the oboe melody in the first few bars, then listen to the whole movement and be asked how many times they have heard it in the bass. (Four times.)

Brandenburg Concerto No. 2. First movement
The class should listen to the opening ritornello and then be asked to recognise it in the bass at 88 or they might have the music played to them from about 80–100 and he asked to put up their hands when they recognise it. (This is a long movement and will be a difficult test unless the later entry is isolated in this way.)

Brandenburg Concerto No. 5. Last movement
The class might have the opening two-bar fugal theme played to them on the piano and be asked to sing it. Then they might be asked how often they heard it in the bass between bars 1–78. (Four times.) Alternatively they might be asked to recognise its appearance in the bass in the whole movement. (Eight times.) But this is more difficult.

Suite in B minor for Flute and Strings. Allegro, after the introduction
The opening fugal subject might be played to the class on the piano. The exposition of the fugue (bars 1–47) might then be played and the class could be asked how many times they heard the fugue subject, in *any* part. (Five times, including the redundant entry at 44.)

BEETHOVEN *Piano Concerto No. 3 in C minor. Finale; fugal entries at the beginning of the development section, first 20 bars*
The class might be asked how many fugal entries they heard in these twenty bars. (Four.)

Leonora Overture No. 3
(*a*) Bars 154–62. Recognise imitations. (A general question.)

(*b*) Play the theme at the beginning of the allegro (Bars 37–40), with its imitation in the treble a bar later; and then ask for its recognition in the bass at 252, with its imitation in the treble a bar later, by playing a longer passage to include it (240–64 or 271?).

Symphony No. 3 in E flat (Eroica). First movement
Play the opening theme on the piano or on the record. Then play 178–206 and ask how many times these two bars are played in the bass. (Ten times.)

Symphony No. 6 in F (Pastoral). Third movement. Bars 165–203.
Play 165–8 on the piano; then ask how many times it appears, partially or complete, in the bass, in this passage. (Five times.)

Symphony No. 8 in F major. First movement
Tell the class that the first subject reappears in the bass at the beginning of the recapitulation and ask them to put up their hands when this happens (Bar 190). Then listen to the whole movement.

BERLIOZ *Carnival Romaine Overture. Bars 21–60*
Tell the class they are going to hear a theme in the cor anglais, which later returns in the violas (37); and later again in the 'cellos (53). Ask for their recognition in some way. They might also be asked to recognise the canon between violin and 'cello, starting at 61 and continuing to 66.

BRITTEN *Young Person's Guide to the Orchestra*
If the class listens to the whole of this work they can be asked to put up their hands when they hear the Purcell theme return near the end, combined with Britten's fugue. (Fourteen bars after M.)

DVORAK *Symphony No. 5 in E minor (The New World). First movement*
Second subject, Figure 3 and the following 21 bars. Ask the class to put up their hands when they hear the theme reappear (*a*) in the middle of the texture (nine bars later), and (*b*) at the bottom of the texture (seventeen bars later).

HAYDN *String Quartet in B flat major, Op. 50, No. 1. Minuet to the first double bar.*
Ask for recognition of the theme when it is heard in the 'cellos (Bar 9).

String Quartet in D major, Op. 64, No. 5. Minuet, bars 1–16
Recognise return of theme in second violins (9) and 'cellos (12).

Symphony No. 99 in E flat. Finale. Bars 1–20
Recognise the return of the theme in 'cellos and then violas at 13 and 15, followed by modifications of it in the violins at 17.

Symphony No. 101 in D (The Clock). Finale
Play opening theme. Then hear 189–218 and ask how many times they hear it and what instruments play it. (189, violins; 193, violins; 198, 'cellos; 203, violins; 205, violas; 212, violins).

Symphony No. 102 *in B flat. First movement*

Play second subject ('cellos, last beat of 56–60) on the piano. Then let the class hear 160–84 and ask for comments. (A canon in three parts.)

HOLST *St. Paul's Suite for Strings. Finale*
Recognise 'Greensleeves' under 'Dargason'.

MOZART *Clarinet Quintet. Trio II*
Recognise the theme of trio II at bars 104–8, when it is heard in the 'cellos.
Overture to the 'Magic Flute'. Allegro
Bars 16–43. Recognise the first subject when it occurs in the bass at 27, 33 and 41. Also bars 103–27, when the first two bars of it occur at 105, 109, 117, 119, 121 and 123. Similarly bars 146–58, when one bar of it occurs in rising sequences at 149, 150, 151 and 152; and two bars of it at 156–7.
Symphony in E flat, K.543. Finale. Development section, 109–35
Recognise first bar of first subject in the bass at 116, 118, 120, 122 and 124 —133, all in imitation of the violins.
Symphony in G minor, K.550. First movement. Development section, 101–38.
First subject in the bass at 115 and 123.
Recapitulation, 191–211
Notice the theme in the violins at 191, and then recognsie it in the bass at 198.
Menuetto
Notice the three entries of the theme in the bass after the double bar.
Symphony in C major, K. 551 (Jupiter). Finale
Play first four bars of first subject. Then listen to 36–55, saying how many times these bars recur. (Six times.)
(This is a complicated movement; but, if the teacher thinks his class can cope with it, he can give them all the four main themes, A, B, C, D, and then ask them to notice how they are combined in the coda.)

SCHUBERT *String Quartet in A minor, Op.* 29. *First movement*
Bars 119–30. Recognise the canon between 'cello and first violin.
Piano Quintet, Op. 114 *(The Trout). Variation movement*
Compare theme and variation III, recognizing the theme in the bass.
Octet, Op. 166. *Second movement. Bars* 1–36
Recognise the first subject in the bass at 25.

TSCHAIKOVSKY *Symphony No.* 5 *in E minor (The New World). Second movement*
Bars 1–43. Recognise the first subject when it recurs at 33 in the 'cellos.

WAGNER *Mastersingers Overture*
(*a*) Recognise the first subject in the brass at 151.
(*b*) If all the themes have been learnt by the class they can listen to the

passage starting at 158, when the 'Prize Song', the 'Mastersingers' March and the Apprentices' theme in diminution all occur together, the 'Mastersingers' theme being in the bass.

(b) *Recognition of a well-known hidden melody in the bass*

This test differs from test (*a*) in that the class has not just previously heard the tune they are to recognise in its new guise. The teacher should be sure that the tune is likely to be known by the class; but this is, in effect, a guessing game, which will be enjoyed by the class, while, at the same time, it has educational value.

The hidden tunes given below are grouped into categories three or four to each category. The teacher can, if he wishes, state the category; or he can withhold all information, leaving the pupil to recognise the tune purely by its sound. If it is not recognised the first time the teacher may play it a second or even a third time, a little louder in relation to its counter-melody or harmony.

Sometimes the pupil may recognise the melody but be momentarily unable to name it. In that case he should give as much information about it as he can, thus proving that he recognises its sound.

The teacher can, if he wishes, disguise some of the tunes which are part of a prescribed work, in a similar way.

Hymns

1   *O worship the King*

2   *Praise, my Soul, the King of Heaven*

3   *Ye holy Angels bright*

246

4

Carols

5   Allegro

The Holly and the Ivy

6   Allegro

The First Nowell

7   Andante

Silent Night

247

8 Andante

Emperor's Hymn Haydn

9 Largo

Largo Handel

10 Allegro

Hark! Hark! the Lark Schubert

11 **Moderato** *On Wings of Song* Mendelssohn

European Folk Songs

12 **Pesante** *Volga Boat Song*

13 **Vivace** *Sur le pont d'Avignon*

249

14 Moderato

Die Lorelei

15 Allegro

La Marseillaise

American Folk Songs

16 Allegro

Clementine

17 Allegro

John Brown's Body

Swing low, sweet chariot

18 Andante

English Folk Songs

19 Moderato

Begone dull care

20 Allegro moderato

This Old Man

21 Moderato

22 Andante

23 Moderato

24 Lento   *Ye Banks and Braes*

poco rit.

Welsh Folk Songs   *The Ash Grove*
25 Moderato

26 Allegro   *Rise, Rise, thou merry Lark*

27 Andante   *All through the night*

Irish Folk Songs

28   Moderato

Cockles and Mussels

29   Andante

The Minstrel Boy

30   Andante

The Harp that once

11 Recognition of themes from works which have been previously studied

This test can take one of three forms. The first two are more commonly required for C.S.E., while the third is more usual for G.C.E. As the method of preparation for them is rather different they are considered separately here.

(a) Recognition of themes by ear alone

The candidate must know the prescribed works really well. But the themes to be recognised are likely to be only the main ones, and the information will not be required in great detail. The pupil should be trained to give the answer in tabular form and always in the same way. For example (a) Mozart, *G Minor Symphony*. Second movement. First subject. (b) Tschaikovsky, *Romeo and Juliet*. The Friar's theme, or the fight between the Montagues and the Capulets.

If the second subject of a work for orchestra in sonata form is given for recognition and the orchestration in the exposition and the recapitulation is different, then a recognition of the difference might reasonably be expected. For example: in Mendelssohn's *Hebrides Overture* the second subject starts in the 'cello in the exposition and in the clarinet in the recapitulation. The candidate could be expected to state: Mendelssohn, *Hebrides Overture*. The second subject as it occurs in the recapitulation, played by the clarinet.

But differences between the statement of a theme in the exposition and the development section when the difference is mainly one of key; or between the second subject in exposition and recapitulation of a movement for piano when the key is again the main difference, would not be expected to be recognised aurally in the C.S.E. And subsidiary themes are not likely to be given unless they have a special significance, such as that of the trumpet call off stage in Beethoven's *Leonora Overture No. 3*.

(b) Recognition of themes which are given both aurally and visually

This should be easier than (a). The candidate has the themes printed in front of him and probably has time to study them before they are heard. Certainly he can follow the melody as it is played.

The number of works prescribed for study in C.S.E. examinations varies from one to twenty or more. If only a few are given the resourceful candidate has a useful method of checking his answers. He can make a list of the key, tempo and time signature of each work or movement from a work beforehand. Then, if he sees a quotation in E major, *allegro* in $\frac{6}{8}$ time, it is quite possible that this can only apply to one work. Even if there are two or three to which this applies, the possibilities are narrowed considerably; and hearing the quotation should settle the question.

If only a few works are prescribed and scores have been used, or if one work has to be studied in detail with the score, it may also be reasonable to expect candidates to recognise the difference between the second subject in the exposition and the recapitulation by means of the key. And passages such as the last few bars of the *Hebrides Overture* could reasonably be expected to be recognised.

The method of setting out the answer suggested in (*a*) above should still be followed, though the candidate should add as much further information as he can as, for example, the exact position in the work, or details of the scoring.

(*c*) *Recognition of themes by sight alone*

This is much the most difficult of the three methods, and is the one usually given for both O and A Level in G.C.E.

It assumes that a candidate can look at a melody on a piece of paper and can turn it into sound in his head.

He should first look at the speed mark and then mentally sing the rhythm at this speed. If he sings a quick rhythm slowly or a slow rhythm quickly he may be completely misled.

Then he should look at the key signature, look for indications as to whether it is in a major or minor key, and then sing the melody in his head, in the rhythm and at the speed previously decided upon, being sure to start on the right note of the scale.

Sol-fa names and rhythm names are a great help in this work, provided that the student is really familiar with them and can translate them into sound. (I have marked an examination paper in which the candidate had written the sol-fa names over every melody to be identified and yet had been unable to name one of them! This is much more likely to have been due to the lack of link between sol-fa syllables and sound than to a lack of knowledge of the themes. If the melody had been played as well, as in (*b*) above, he would probably have found no difficulty.)

If the candidate knows his set-works he should now be able to identify the theme, and to state the facts about it in the order suggested in (*a*) and (*b*) above.

He will again find it useful to make a note of the keys, speed and time signatures of the main themes, by this means narrowing the possibilities of recognition of any particular theme.

If he has time it is better still to keep a manuscript book in which he writes all the main themes, thus learning the themes and also learning to link sight with sound. By this means he will also become aware of key, speed and time signature, as suggested above; and he should make a note of such things as the two keys of the second subject in exposition and recapitulation, and possibly also of an important appearance of a theme in a different key in the development section of a movement.

If the list of melodies for recognition includes some which are not in the particular set works the candidate has studied, then he should be able to dismiss them at once, on the ground that he has studied no movement in the particular key, tempo, or time signature as that shown.

This requirement is therefore a test of two equally important, yet separate things: the ability to turn sight into sound; and a thorough knowledge of the prescribed works.

256

Section XII
Tests of General Musical Literacy

These are types of tests which are being encouraged by the Department of Education and Science, in particular for the C.S.E. examination.

There are fourteen Examining Boards for the C.S.E., and several of these contain two divisions, such as North and South, which set different syllabuses. Frequent changes are, at present, being made in these syllabuses; and, in addition, any school or group of schools is free to produce its own syllabus and prepare candidates for it. So it is obviously unwise to state here that a particular test is required for a particular examination, though it is hoped that all types of these tests are covered in this book.

Some C.S.E. Boards include simple rhythm, pitch, cadence or chord tests of the kinds given in earlier Sections of this book.

But, in addition, most Boards give what the Department calls 'Tests of individual listening'. They are covered in the various parts of this Section. Some Boards ask for one thing at a time. Others ask for several things at the same time. The latter is certainly more difficult; and it is therefore advisable for the teacher to begin by dealing with each kind of test separately, as is shown in parts 1–7 below. Part 8 contains a number of varied questions on the same piece of music.

All these tests have one thing in common: the candidate is given a sheet of music paper containing an incomplete melody, and he has to add various things to it to complete it, or possibly to alter it, after he has heard it played several times.

At present, the teacher has little ready-made material for these tests. He has the Department's specimen records and the few tests set by his own Examining Board in previous years. Otherwise he must prepare his own, and provide pupils with copies, and all this takes time. The tests which follow below should prove useful, though the teacher will still have to provide his pupils with copies. And, based on these tests, he can make up further material of the same kind.

In addition to aural discrimination, the student requires to know a certain amount of musical theory before working these tests. This can all be found in the author's *Basic Music Knowledge* under the relevant headings. Also there are many melodies in that book that can be adapted as additional material for this Section.

In parts 1–6 of this Section the material which has to be added by the pupil is printed in red. In part 7 the altered versions played by the teacher are given in red. In part 8 the complete melody played by the teacher is given in red.

257

The teacher must therefore prepare copies for his pupils to work, with some of the material omitted in parts 1–7, and according to the instructions given in part 8. The class can work individually; or, alternatively, the given melody and instructions can be written on the blackboard and the class can work as a team. The latter may save the teacher's time, and should be helpful in the early stages, as each point can be discussed with the teacher. But the pupils should eventually have *some* practice in working individually; so cyclostyled or photostat copies will be necessary.

As these tests are all melodies, they can be played on the piano by the teacher. But, in the actual examination, they may be given on a gramophone record or tape.

1 Adding speed and expression marks to a melody

(Section 5 of the author's *Basic Music Knowledge* gives all the terms required under this heading.)

The student should be given a list of speed marks from which to choose. Otherwise such a test is impossible to mark. For instance, in test number 1, given *presto*, *allegretto* or *adagio*, *allegretto* is the only possible one. But if the student was left to choose *any* suitable speed mark, all the following would be possible: *vivace*, *allegro moderato*, *allegretto*, *moderato*, *andante con moto*, *scherzando*.

Similarly with expression marks:——————, *cresc*, *sf*. > , and ⌒ are all, at times, interchangeable; and it is difficult to distinguish between *mp* and *mf*. So the student needs to be given a list of expression marks to insert at suitable places.

1. Add *presto*, *allegretto* or *adagio* at the beginning of the following song to indicate its speed. Also add *p*.——————, *rit*, ⌒ , and *a tempo*, in this order, at suitable places.

2. Add *vivace*, *lento* or *andante con moto* to indicate the speed of the following song. Also add *mf*, *sf*, *p*, and *cresc*, in this order, at suitable places.

258

3. Add *prestissimo*, *largo* or *andantino* at the beginning of this extract to indicate its speed. Then add *p* (twice), *f* (twice), ⌢ , *a tempo*, *ad lib*, and *molto rall* at suitable places, not necessarily in this order.

Oh! rest thee, babe Whittaker

Oh! rest thee, my dar-ling, the time it shall come, When thy sleep shall be broken by

trum-pet and drum: Then rest thee, my dar-ling, Oh! sleep while you may. For

war comes with manhood as light comes with day. Oh! rest thee, babe, rest thee, babe

sleep on till day,— Oh! rest thee, babe rest thee, babe, sleep while you may.

4. Add *allegro moderato*, *largo* or *andante* as a suitable speed mark at the beginning of the following song. Then add *p*'s and *f*'s, pauses, *rit*, > , *con anima*, and *cresc* at suitable places.

Blow high, blow low Dibdin

Blow high, blow low, let tem-pests tear the main-mast by the board: My

heart with thoughts of thee, my dear, And love well stored. Shall

brave all dan-ger scorn all fear, The roar-ing winds, the ra-ging sea. In

hopes or shore to be once more safe moored with thee.

5. The following expression marks have been used by the composer in this song, though not in this order. Insert them in their correct places: *pp*, *p*, *mf*, <> , *allegretto*, ⌢ , *dim*, > (twice), *dolce e tranquillo*.

A lovely evening in summer 'twas Grieg

6. Add one of the following to this extract as a suitable speed mark: *andantino, allegro molto, prestissimo.* Then add *f, sf, p, f, decresc,* and ⌢ (in this order); and slurs and staccato dots where you think they come.

Finale of the Eroica Symphony Beethoven

7. Add *allegro, adagio* or *andante* as a suitable speed mark to this extract. Then add the following expression marks (not necessarily in this order): *p* (5 times), *f* (twice), *sf,* ⤜⤛, ⌢ , *dim, pp.*

Second movement of the London Symphony Haydn

8. Add *largo, vivace* or *moderato* as a speed mark to the following extract. Then, by means of slurs, staccato dots and ⤛ show how it is played.

Finale from quartet Op.74 No.1 Haydn

9. Add *adagio, moderato* or *presto* as a suitable speed mark to this extract. The following expression marks appear, most of them several times, and not necessarily in this order. Add them where you think they come: *p, f,* ⤜⤛, *pp, ten,* slurs and phrase marks.

Fantasia Mozart

2 Showing the structure of a melody

This can take the form of adding phrase marks to a melody; adding letters, A, B, etc., showing its structure; naming its form; marking sequences or other kinds of development or variation; naming the keys of the various sections; recognising the cadences; or a mixture of all of these.

The information given in the author's *Basic Music Knowledge*, Section 2, parts 1–3 and 6–7; Section 3, parts 1–5 and 8–11; Section 6; Section 10; Section 11, part 22, and Section 15, parts 2–3 and 5–6 could, with advantage, be studied before working this section. Section 6 should be particularly useful. But, although the facts given there need to be known, the exercises in this book are rather easier because the student hears the melody being played while the copy is in front of him.

It is assumed that he has learnt to follow music from a copy, and that he can hear the breaks between phrases and knows how to show them by means of phrase marks. He should not confuse bar lines with phrase marks (a very common error) but should realise how often a phrase begins anacrusically and ends in the middle of a bar. He should expect phrases to be normally two or four bars long; and his eye should help his ear and memory in recognising the repetition or modified repetition of a phrase.

1. Add phrase marks to this melody. Then label the phrases A, B, etc. Name the key. What kind of a cadence occurs at the end?

2. Continue with the phrasing of this melody, and give each phrase its appropriate label. Name the key. Also name the cadences marked with a bracket.

3. Phrase the rest of this melody and add the label A each time the first phrase appears. There is a sequence in this melody. Write 'seq' under the phrase marks concerned.

4. Continue the phrase marks in this extract, and mark 'seq' every time a sequence occurs. Name the key.

The Leather Bottel Old English

5. Phrase the rest of this melody. Mark 'seq' where a sequence occurs. By reference to bar numbers point out two examples of repetition.

Wandering Schubert

4^4–8^3 is a repetition of the beginning –4^3.
14^4–16^3 is a repetition of 12^4–14^3.

6. In this extract some phrases are two bars long and others last for only one bar. Phrase it throughout. Mark any sequences; and name the key at the beginning and end of the extract.

We all love a pretty girl Arne

7. Compare the two halves of this extract, and name the key of each half.

The Minstrel's Song Grieg

The two halves are identical except that the first half is in C major, and the second half in A♭ major.

8. (*a*) Phrase this tune throughout.
   (*b*) Name the form of the tune as a whole.
   (*c*) Compare 4^3–8^1 with the beginning to 4^2.
   (*d*) In what key does the tune begin and end?
   (*e*) In what key is the tune at bars 8^3–12^1?

To Alexis Hummel

(b) Ternary form.

(c) 4^3–8^1 is an octave higher than the beginning to 4^2.

(d) The tune begins and ends in G major.

(e) It is in D major at bars 8^3–12^1.

9. Phrase this song throughout. Then add labels (A, B, etc.) to denote the form and name the form of the song.

The Plough Boy Old English

10. (a) Phrase this tune throughout.

(b) Compare bars 1–2 with 9–11.

(c) Compare 1–11 with 12–22.

(d) How would you describe 22^4–5?

Forget-me-not Köhler

(b) Bars 1 and 9 are identical. Bars 10 and 11 are an augmentation of bar 2.

(c) Bars 12–23 are a decoration or variation of bars 1–11.

(d) Bars 22^4–25 form a coda.

3 Adding time signatures and bar lines to an unbarred melody

This is primarily a test of being able to hear the relative strength of notes and putting a bar line before every strong accent. This must be done by means of aural perception, not mathematical reasoning. 'A bar line is a thing you hear' can never be said too often to students.

All the tests except the first one given below have some of the beats divided into smaller sections. So the next thing the students must listen for is whether the beats divide into two or three (simple or compound time).

If they decide that the time is simple then the signature will probably be $\frac{2}{4}$, $\frac{3}{4}$ or $\frac{4}{4}$, though they may find an occasional division of the beat into three (see No. 9); an occasional mixture of times (see No. 11); or even, very rarely, $\frac{5}{4}$ time (see No. 12). If No. 10 is played fast enough they should realise that the minim is the beat and that the time signature is $\frac{2}{2}$.

If they hear that most or all of the beats are divisible into three then the time, in this easy kind of test, will be $\frac{6}{8}$.

Only after the bar lines have been put in and the note values grouped into beats should students let 'counting' come into the matter, deciding by this means the number of beats in the bar and the resulting time signature.

Of course, students must be acquainted with the most frequently-used time patterns, in both simple and compound time. They should also know that a tie, rather than a dotted note, is used to extend a note over a bar line (see No. 5); and that a semibreve rest is used for a whole bar even in $\frac{2}{4}$, $\frac{3}{4}$ or $\frac{6}{8}$ time (see No. 6). A study of Section I of the author's *Basic Music Knowledge* will be useful.

The following tests are graded roughly in order of difficulty. In all of them the students have to add bar lines and then time signatures. The teacher can easily find more material of the same kind, if required.

4 Completing a melody of which the pitch and bar lines are given

The information and training for this test is all given in Section II. But the tests given here are of a different and rather easier kind because the bar lines and the pitch (and therefore the number) of notes are given. They might be worked side by side with Section II though, in that case, the teacher must be careful that the tests given here do not go beyond the knowledge of the student.

There is no doubt, however, that the safest and surest way of learning to use and understand rhythmic notation is by working through as much of Section II as is required. If the teacher desires he can give the pitch of the tests in Section II, as is done here.

It is certainly easier to confine the student's attention to one thing at a time (in this case, the time pattern) as in Section II and the tests given here, than to expect him to listen to other things at the same time, as, for example, in writing a complete melody or working part 8 of this Section.

The pitch and bar lines of the following melodies should be given to the pupil, either on the blackboard or on individual pieces of paper, and he should add connecting lines joining together notes belonging to the same beat, stems, rests, hooks, dots and ties, or turn black dots into minims, etc., according to what he hears. He should be careful to put the stems and hooks the right side of the notes, and the right way up.

5 Completing a melody of which the rhythm is given

Part 5 below bears the same relationship to Sections III and IV that part 4 of this Section did to Section II. In other words, it would be an advantage to work some of Sections III and IV, following the advice given there about method of working, before studying this part. But the exercises in this part are considerably easier than most of those in Section IV, for not only is the rhythm of each test given but the melodies vary from very easy to easy, and no tests are given in a minor key. Stepwise movement, sometimes combined with leaps between notes of the doh chord, predominates; and the tests are of the easy type that might be given in C.S.E.

The teacher can, if he wishes, dictate some of the tests in Section IV, parts 1 and 2, giving the rhythm beforehand, and working them side by side with the tests in this part.

The teacher should give the rhythm *above* the stave, leaving the students to write the correct notes in this rhythm *on* the stave. He may, if necessary, give the first note, or the notes of an occasional awkward leap, to the students in the early stages.

The tests are graded, roughly in order of difficulty. A long test, such as Nos. 10 and 15, may prove difficult because of its length, even though the notes themselves are easy. But the number of times each test is dictated, and the length given of each section, is a matter for the teacher to decide, bearing in mind the particular examination for which he is preparing.

Müller

Trio from Symphony No.2 Beethoven

The Sandman Brahms

Trio from Sonata in A Mozart

The Death of Nelson Braham

Sonata in A Mozart

London Symphony Haydn

Lovely Cradle of my sorrows Schumann

Humming Song Schumann

Finale of Symphony No.9 Beethoven

Lord at all times, I will bless Thee Mendelssohn

May Dew Sterndale Bennett

Serenade Schumann

Sapphic Ode Brahms

Rigadon Purcell

6 Completing a melody, part of which is given

Part 6 is really a combination of parts 4 and 5. The student has to write both rhythm and pitch; but the tests are easier than those in Section IV because he is given part of each melody, which provides a good indication of how it is likely to continue. The part he has to add may contain a sequence or a repetition of a phrase previously given; and even when this is not the case, the required addition is always easy. The standard is, again, that of C.S.E., so there are no examples in a minor key, though three (Nos. 9, 12 and 14) are in compound time.

The student should listen keenly to the part he is given and compare it with the part to be added, being alert to notice sequences and repetitions. He should also be particularly careful about the joins.

The tests are roughly in order of difficulty.

I am a friar of Orders Grey Reeve

Minuet Rameau

Trumpet Tune Grano

Begone, dull Care Old English

Trio from String Quartet Op.33 No.2 Haydn

Romance in G Beethoven

Gaily the troubadour Bayley

7 Detecting discrepancies between a copy of a melody and its performance

This is another C.S.E. test and is very useful, because it proves whether a student is able to link notation accurately with sound. Yet it is comparatively easy because all the student has to do is to locate the changes listed; he is not required to write down the notes of the changed version.

A melody is placed in front of the student and it is played once exactly as written. Then two, three or four changes are made at subsequent performances of the melody (all the changes taking place at each performance, which is usually three times) and he has to mark on the copy where these changes have been made.

The changes are listed below the copy (or told verbally to the student), and labelled (*a*), (*b*), etc. He therefore puts (*a*), (*b*) over the changed bars in their correct places.

271

The original version of each melody is given in full below, and the altered versions are written in small print above each changed bar. They correspond to the information given to the student ((*a*), (*b*), etc.), though they are not necessarily in the same order.

Blow, blow thou winter Wind Arne

(*a*) A lower note.
(*b*) A different time pattern, but with the same number of notes.

Hunting Song Schumann

(*a*) Two different notes.
(*b*) More notes in the bar.
(*c*) A different time pattern, but with the same number of notes.

Tom Bowling Dibdin

(*a*) More notes in the bar, and a different time pattern.
(*b*) A different time pattern, but with the same number of notes.
(*c*) An extra note in the bar.

Minuet from the 'Clock' Symphony Haydn

(*a*) Fewer notes in the bar.
(*b*) Lower notes than before.
(*c*) Higher notes than before.

Dance from 'Orpheus' Gluck

(a) Three different notes.
(b) Fewer notes than before.
(c) A different time pattern, but with the same number of notes.

The Girl I left behind me Old English

(a) Fewer notes in the bar.
(b) The tune is higher.
(c) The notes move in the opposite direction.

Polonaise in A Chopin

(a) Lower notes.
(b) A different time pattern, but with the same number of notes.
(c) Higher notes.
(d) More notes in the bar.

Cherry Ripe Horn

(a) Three higher notes.
(b) An extra note, combined with a variation in the tune.
(c) A different time pattern, but with the same number of notes.

273

Minuet in G Purcell

(a) Two different notes—higher.
(b) Two different notes—lower.
(c) Two adjacent bars of lower notes.

Should he upraid Bishop

(a) A different time pattern, but with the same number of notes in the bars.
(b) More notes in the bar, making a different pitch and time pattern.
(c) Three higher notes.
(d) Fewer notes in the bar.

8 Answering a number of varied questions on a melody which is played, part of which is given

In these tests a number of varying questions, corresponding more or less to those given separately in parts 1–6 of this Section are asked about the same melody. The melody is played a number of times, and the student is told what to listen for and what to add at each hearing. He can be told verbally, if necessary; but it is better if the student has the questions in front of him and is given time to read them all beforehand.

Nevertheless it is considerably more difficult than listening to one thing at a time; and the best method of preparation is undoubtedly to practise each skill separately by working parts 1–6 above.

The material which the student is given is shown first in each case, followed by the questions he has to answer. The teacher then plays the melody given in full below, as often as the instructions require.

In the C.S.E. examination this melody might be part of a chamber or orchestral work, played on a tape or record; and the questions might include some on the scoring. This is obviously impossible in this Section, in which the teacher plays the melodies on the piano. Such questions have been dealt with in Section. XI of this book, and should not be combined with Section XII. In any case it is even more difficult if the two types of question are combined.

1. The student is supplied with manuscript paper on which is written:

and three lines below, supplied with clefs and key signatures and ten spaced-out bar lines. He is also given the questions.

First hearing. Insert the notes given above, with their correct note values, so that they make the first two bars of the music. Then write in the time signature.

Second hearing. Follow the melody as it is played, and add phrase marks over the top of the staves and a double bar line at the end (which is not necessarily at the end of ten bars).

Third hearing. Add the rhythm of bars 3 and 4, writing it above the staff.

Fourth hearing. Add letters, A, B, etc., to show the shape of the music.

Fifth hearing. Add one of the following as a suitable speed and expression mark: *vivace e leggero; andante maestoso; largo e mesto.* Then add *p*'s and *f*'s where necessary.

Sixth hearing. Add anything more you can of the notation.

2. The student is supplied with manuscript paper on which is written:

and 26 spaced-out bar lines, with clefs and key signatures at the beginning of each line. He is also given the questions.

First hearing. Copy the given notes, with their correct note values, so that they fill the first four bars of the music paper. Then add the time signature.

Second hearing. Add as much as you can of the next four bars (the second phrase).

Third hearing. Add phrase marks throughout and a double-bar line where you think the end comes.

Fourth hearing. Add A, B, etc., to show the shape of the tune, calling the first eight bars A. In what form is the tune?

Fifth hearing. B starts with 𝄞 . Continue as much of it as possible.

Sixth hearing. Add as much more of the notation as you can.

Old Folk Tune

3. The student is supplied with manuscript paper, on which is written the following, and the questions given below.

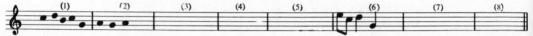

First hearing. Add whatever is necessary to the first eight notes to produce the correct note values. Then add the time signature.

Second hearing. Add the rhythm over the staff up to the end of the fourth bar.

Third hearing. Add the fifth bar, complete with melody and rhythm.

Fourth hearing. Add the rhythm over the staff up to the end.

Fifth hearing. Add the phrase marks throughout.

Sixth hearing. Add whichever of the following you think suits the music: *allegro marcato; adagio e tragico; andante espressivo.* Also add ◁▷ in two suitable places.

Seventh hearing. State the key at the beginning and the end of the extract.

4. The student is supplied with manuscript paper, on which is written:

and 26 bar lines, with clefs and key signatures at the beginning of each line. He is also given the questions.

First hearing. Add as much of the next two bars as possible. Then add the time signature.

Second hearing. Put one phrase mark over the first four bars. Then add the rest of the phrase marks and a double-bar line at the end. (*N.B.* Bar lines do *not* coincide with the phrase marks.)

Third hearing. Calling the first four-bar phrase A, add letters to all the other phrases.

Fourth hearing. B starts [music notation]. Add as much more of it as possible, at the correct place in the tune.

Fifth hearing. Add as much more of the notation as you can.
Sixth hearing. Add four of the following terms at appropriate places: *adagio; allegro; moderato; mf; ff; p; pp, rit.*

In the Garden Köhler

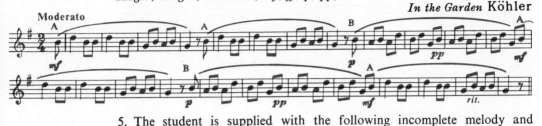

5. The student is supplied with the following incomplete melody and questions:

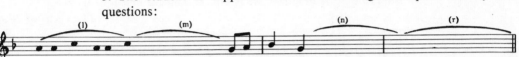

First hearing. Listen to the melody throughout and add the time signature.
Second hearing. Write the correct note values and bar lines at (l).
Third hearing. Write the complete tune at (m).
Fourth hearing. Write the complete tune at (n).
Fifth hearing. Write the rhythm over the top of the staff at (r).
Sixth hearing. Add a suitable dynamic mark at the beginning, and ⏝⏞ where you think it comes. Also add whichever of the following is applicable at the beginning: *con moto tranquillo; presto agitato; adagio.*
Seventh hearing. Say whether each of the endings of the two halves of the tune are masculine or feminine.

Lullaby Brahms

6. The student is supplied with the following incomplete melody and questions:

First hearing. Name the key, write in the time signature, and state whether the extract ends with a perfect or imperfect cadence.
Second hearing. Write the complete tune at (l).
Third hearing. Write the complete tune at (m).
Fourth hearing. Write the rhythm of the two bars at (n).
Fifth hearing. Write *cresc;* and ⎯⎯▷, twice, at suitable places.

Minuet in F Mozart

7. The student is supplied with manuscript paper on which the following is written, together with 16 more spaced-out bar lines, and clefs and key signatures at the beginning of every line. He is also given the questions.

First hearing. Complete the note values and add the bar lines to the following extract. Then add the time signature.

Second and third hearings. Add as much as you can of the next four bars.

Fourth hearing. Add phrase marks throughout the tune and a double-bar line at the end.

Fifth hearing. Add labels, A, B, etc., calling the first four bars A.

The Vicar of Bray

8. The student is supplied with the following incomplete melody and the questions below it.

First hearing. Add bars 5–8.

Second and third hearings. Add bars 17–20.

Fourth and fifth hearings. Add bars 21–4.

Sixth hearing. Compare bars 1–2 with 17–8 and 21–2.

Seventh hearing. Compare 9–16 with 25–32. Why do you think the endings are different?

Köhler

278

9. Give the student manuscript paper on which the following is written, together with 16 spaced-out bar lines, and clefs and key signatures at the beginning of every line. He is also given the list of questions.

First hearing. Add the rhythm of bars 3 and 4 over the top of the staff.
Second hearing. Add the complete melody of bars 5 and 6.
Third hearing. Add the rhythm of bars 7 and 8 over the top of the staff.
Fourth hearing. Add phrase marks throughout, and letters showing its structure.
Fifth hearing. Write the melody of bars 9–12.
Sixth hearing. Add the rhythm to the end of the extract, over the top of the staff.
Seventh hearing. Add either *vivace*, *largo* or *andantino* as a speed mark; a suitable dynamic mark at the beginning; ——————twice; *rit*; and *a tempo*.

***Entracte from Rosamunde* Schubert**

10. The student is given the following incomplete melody and the questions which follow it.

First hearing. Name the key and add the time signature.
Second hearing. Add the phrase marks, and letters, A, B, etc., showing its structure.
Third hearing. Add the complete melody of bar 2.
Fourth hearing. Add the complete melody of bars 5–8 and 13–16.
Fifth hearing. Add the rhythm of bars 9–12 over the top of the staff.
Sixth hearing. Add as much as you can of the melody of bars 9–12.

Drink to me only with thine eyes

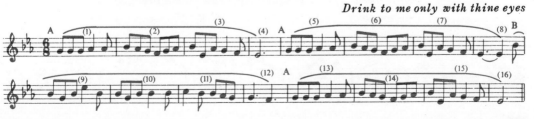

279

11. The student is given the following beginning and 20 spaced-out bar lines, with clefs and key signatures at the beginning of every line. He is also given the questions.

First hearing. Add the correct note values and bar lines of the above extract. (It does *not* begin on the first beat of the bar.) Then add the time signature.
Second hearing. Add the rhythm to complete the first four-bar phrase, over the top of the staff.
Third hearing. Add phrase marks throughout, and a double-bar line at the end.
Fourth hearing. Compare the beginning of each of the four phrases.
Fifth hearing. Write as much as you can of the second phrase.
Sixth hearing. Write as much as you can of the third phrase.
Seventh hearing. State the name of the cadences halfway through and at the end of the tune.
Eighth hearing. Add one of the following as an indication of style: *staccato; tranquillo; marcato.*

12. The student is given the following extract, together with the list of questions.

First hearing. Add bar 3.
Second hearing. Add bar 4.
Third hearing. Add bars 7 and 8.
Fourth hearing. In what key is the extract (*a*) at the beginning; (*b*) at the end?
Fifth hearing. Point out an example of (*a*) sequence; (*b*) repetition, by writing the word over the bar concerned.
Sixth hearing. Add one of the following at the beginning: *allegro con spirito; presto vivace; lento cantabile.* Also add the following at suitable places (not necessarily in this order): *pp; f*, twice; *p;* , twice.

13. The student is given the following, together with 18 spaced-out bar lines, clefs and key signatures at the beginning of every line, and the list of questions.

First hearing. Add note values and bar lines to the given beginning; also add the time signature.

Second and third hearings. Complete the first phrase.

Fourth hearing. Put phrase marks over the whole of the extract and a double-bar line at the end.

Fifth hearing. Add letters, A, B, etc., to show the structure; and add the tune where A is repeated.

Sixth hearing. Add as much more of the melody as you can.

Seventh hearing. Name the cadence (*a*) half-way through; (*b*) at the end.

Rustic Song Schumann

14. The student is given the following incomplete melody and the list of questions.

First hearing. Add the time signature, and get a general impression of the tune.

Second hearing. Complete the end of bar 2 and add the whole of bar 3.

Third hearing. Add bars 5–8.

Fourth hearing. Add bars 9–10.

Fifth hearing. Fill in the gap in bars 13 and 14, and name the device which is used there.

Sixth hearing. Add one of the following as a speed mark: *presto; moderato; largo;* and the following expression marks at suitable places: *f, p, ⌒* (twice), *cresc.*

The Bay of Biscay Davy

15. Give the student the following beginning, together with 16 spaced-out bar lines and the list of questions.

First hearing. Add note lengths to the first bar; and add the time signature.
Second hearing. Add the second bar.
Third and fourth hearings. Add the third and fourth bars.
Fifth hearing. Add phrase marks throughout, and a double-bar line at the end.
Sixth hearing. Add letters, A, B, etc. Then copy in the tune of A where it re-occurs, using the sign 8va where necessary.
Seventh hearing. Add the first two bars of B.
Eighth hearing. Add the rhythm of the next two bars over the top of the staff.

Sonatina **Schmitt**

16. Give the student the following bars on a sheet of music paper, and the list of questions.

First hearing. Copy the given opening, with its correct note values, and add the time signature.
Second hearing. Write in the next complete bar.
Third hearing. Write the rhythm of bars 3 and 4 over the top of the staff.
Fourth hearing. Add phrase marks throughout the melody, letters to indicate its structure, and a double-bar line at the end.
Fifth hearing. Write bars 5 and 6 complete.
Sixth hearing. Write the rhythm of the last two bars over the top of the staff.
Seventh hearing. Add as much more of the melody as you can.
Eighth hearing. Name the cadences at the end of bar 4 and bar 8.

Love has eyes **Bishop**

17. Give the student the following incomplete extract and the questions relating to it.

First hearing. Add the correct note values to bar 1, and the time signature.
Second and third hearings. Add bars 2 and 3.
Fourth hearing. Add bar 6.
Fifth hearing. Point out any examples of sequences by writing 'seq.' over the top.
Sixth hearing. Name the key (*a*) at the beginning; (*b*) at the end of the extract.
Seventh hearing. Choose the most suitable of the following and place it at the beginning as a speed and expression mark: *andante cantabile; presto furioso; allegretto grazioso.* Then add *mf, pp* (twice),⎯⎯, and *dim* at suitable places in the passage.

18. Give the student the following beginning on a sheet of music paper and the accompanying questions.

First hearing. Add note values and bar lines to the above extract and add the time signature.
Second hearing. Add the rhythm to the end of the first phrase over the top of the staff.
Third and fourth hearings. Add as much as you can of the next two bars (the second phrase).
Fifth and sixth hearings. Add the rhythm of the rest of the tune above the staff.
Seventh and eighth hearings. Add the melody of as much as you can of this second half of the extract.
Ninth hearing. Name the key (*a*) at the beginning; (*b*) at the end of the extract.

The Heaving of the Lead Shield

283

19. Give the student the following incomplete extract, and the questions relating to it.

First hearing. Add the correct note values of the first six notes, and add the time signature.

Second hearing. Add the melody at (1).

Third hearing. Add the melody at (m).

Fourth hearing. Point out two examples of sequence.

Fifth hearing. Compare the beginnings of the two halves of the extract.

Sixth hearing. Write out the trill in full.

Seventh hearing. Name the cadences (a) half-way through; (b) at the end. Say, in each case, whether they produce masculine or feminine endings.

Eighth hearing. Add suitable speed and expression marks.

Rondo from Sonata in B♭ Mozart

20. Give the student the following incomplete extract and the questions relating to it.

First hearing. Add the time signature and complete the phrase marks.

Second hearing. Add the second phrase up to bar 4.

Third hearing. Add the rhythm over the staff between bars 6 and 8.

Fourth hearing. Add the melody at bars 11 and 12.

Fifth hearing. Add the melody at bar 14, first two beats.

Sixth hearing. Add the rhythm over the staff at bars 14–16.

Seventh hearing. Add the melody from bar 18 to the end.

Eighth hearing. Add as much more of the notation as you can.

Ninth hearing. Add one of the following at the beginning: *adagio; presto; moderato.*

Tenth hearing. Point out any examples of sequences, by reference to bar numbers.

Eleventh hearing. Compare the last four bars with the four bars immediately preceding them.

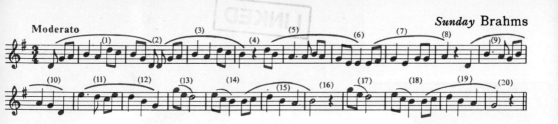